A Conspectus of Scribal Hands Writing English, 700–1100

DONALD SCRAGG

D. S. BREWER

First published 2021
D. S. Brewer, Cambridge

ISBN 978–1–84384–617–8

D. S. Brewer is an imprint of Boydell & Brewer Ltd
PO Box 9, Woodbridge, Suffolk IP12 3DF, UK
and of Boydell & Brewer Inc,
668 Mt Hope Avenue, Rochester, NY 14620–2731, USA
website: www.boydellandbrewer.com

A CIP catalogue record for this book is available
from the British Library

The publisher has no responsibility for the continued existence or accuracy of URLs for external or third-party internet websites referred to in this book,
and does not guarantee that any content on such websites is, or will remain, accurate or appropriate

This publication is printed on acid-free paper

Printed and bound by TJ Books Limited

For Tim

Contents

Preface

I originally designed the predecessor of this volume (*A Conspectus of Scribal Hands Writing English, 960–1100*, published in 2012) as a stepping-stone towards a history of late Old English spelling, and as such its scope was limited to manuscripts and documents generally ascribed to the latter half of the tenth century and the entirety of the eleventh. That projected history having now been abandoned, I felt there would be value in expanding the *Conspectus* by taking the starting date back to the year 700, thereby allowing for the inclusion of around 300 new entries.

For ease of reference, I have retained the layout of the 960–1100 volume, with holding libraries listed alphabetically and individual hands numbered sequentially. To preserve the sequence, new entries have been inserted into the list with a decimal point in the hand number (e.g. 298 Chichester, 298.5 Cologne, 299 Copenhagen). Hand 671 (previously blank) has been added, and hand 1004 has been changed to 1005.2; otherwise, the hand numbers from the 960-1100 volume are unchanged. In places, discontinuous numbering of the decimal points has been used to allow for further additions by future scholars and, particularly in the case of some continental libraries, to allow for future discoveries. Errors that occurred during the composition of the earlier volume have been silently corrected, sporadic instances of English in Latin charters have been noted, and more information regarding facsimiles has been supplied (particularly in relation to the more recent volumes in the Anglo-Saxon Manuscripts in Microfiche Facsimile series, which have useful bibliographies). 'App' before a number in the column listing Ker numbers is now used to signify an entry in his Appendix. In the apparatus, a small number of new entries has been incorporated into the Indices of Names and Places and the Subject Index has also been expanded to accommodate new material. The Appendix to the 2012 volume has been omitted, however, in that it has no bearing on the present work.

Unchanged and unchanging is my debt to Simon Keynes for his assistance with charters, and my appreciation of the unremitting helpfulness and patience shown to me by everyone at Boydell, especially Caroline Palmer. Above all, words cannot convey my gratitude for the help given to me by my son Tim, without whose assistance, when I became too ill for sustained academic work, this project could never have come to fruition.

D. G. S.   2021

Procedures and Conventions

Hand numbers. Lower case letters after numbers suggest either contrary arguments among authorities about the number of hands involved, or my own uncertainty about whether differences are the result of a change of hand or a new stint by the same hand at a different time. Within each number, all manuscripts and documents thought to have been written by the same hand are listed in alphabetical order of libraries.

Libraries and shelf-marks. These are strictly alphabetical, hence Cambridge University Library follows individual Cambridge colleges, in contrast to the procedures of Ker and Gneuss, and Trinity College Cambridge O shelves precede R shelves, against common practice. 'BL' signifies British Library. The + sign links parts of manuscripts now in more than one location which are believed to be part of a single book.

Gneuss numbers are to entries in Gneuss and Lapidge's *Anglo-Saxon Manuscripts*.[1]

Ker numbers are to entries in Ker's *Catalogue*.[2] 'S' after a number indicates a reference to Ker's own Supplement and 'B' indicates Blockley's further additions. 'G' followed by a number represents the addenda supplied by Helmut Gneuss, 'More Old English from Manuscripts', the number representing the item in that list.

Sawyer / Pelteret numbers. Sawyer references are to entries in Sawyer's *Anglo-Saxon Charters*.[3] Pelteret numbers, preceded by P, are to entries in Pelteret's *Catalogue*.[4]

Ker hand no. When Ker assigns numbers to individual scribal hands in his Catalogue entries, those numbers are shown here, since in such instances there is usually a full description of the hands.

Folios. Folio numbers and, where appropriate, line numbers are listed for all but the main hands of large manuscripts. Line numbers for single-page documents are generally omitted. Manuscripts numbered in pages (largely those in Corpus Christi College Cambridge) are signalled by p(p).

Date. Dates are usually palaeographic, by quarter century, and in general follow those in Ker's *Catalogue* or Sawyer / Pelteret. For an explanation, see Ker, *Catalogue*, pp. xx–xxi.

Location. I have striven to locate scribal hands where possible, recognizing that this is the most uncertain element of the Conspectus since scribes were mobile and the distinction between where a document or manuscript was made and where it spent its early years is both a fine one and ultimately incapable of proof. Even when the location of a manuscript is fairly certain, there is no assurance that the scribes involved received their training at the same place. A good example lies in the many scribes who produced London, BL, Royal 7 C XII at the monastery of Cerne in Dorset: although it would appear that the manuscript was written there, its initial writing and many alterations all occurred within a year or so of the founding of the monastery, and the principal scribes probably came from elsewhere. A plentiful use of question

[1] Helmut Gneuss and Michael Lapidge, *Anglo-Saxon Manuscripts* (Toronto, 2014).
[2] N. R. Ker, *Catalogue of Manuscripts Containing Anglo-Saxon* (Oxford, 1957). Towards the end of his life, Ker added to his *Catalogue* with 'A Supplement to *Catalogue of Manuscripts Containing Anglo-Saxon*', *Anglo-Saxon England* 5 (1976), 121–31, and this in turn was subsequently expanded by Mary Blockley, 'Addenda and Corrigenda to N. R. Ker's "A Supplement to Catalogue of Manuscripts Containing Anglo-Saxon"', *Notes and Queries* ns 29 (1982), 1–3, revised and reprinted as 'Further Addenda and Corrigenda to N. R. Ker's *Catalogue*', *Anglo-Saxon Manuscripts: Basic Readings*, ed. Mary P. Richards (New York and London, 1994), pp. 79–85. Further discoveries from the following ten years are described in Helmut Gneuss, 'More Old English from Manuscripts', *Intertexts: Studies in Anglo-Saxon Culture Presented to Paul Szarmach*, ed. Virginia Blanton and Helene Scheck, Medieval and Renaissance Texts and Studies 334 (Tempe, AZ, 2008), pp. 411–21.

[3] P. H. Sawyer, *Anglo-Saxon Charters: An Annotated List and Bibliography*, Royal Historical Society Guides and Handbooks 8 (London, 1968), now revised, updated and expanded by Susan Kelly and others in an electronic form. It is intended that the latter will ultimately be available in book form..
[4] David A. E. Pelteret, *Catalogue of English Post-Conquest Vernacular Documents* (Woodbridge, 1990).

marks in the location column gives evidence of the difficulty of reaching certainty on this subject when such a large part of written material from the period is lost. Nevertheless the exercise of listing such locations as are known or supposed and indexing them seems worthwhile since it may well give rise to further scholarship on this most vexed subject, and an ability to identify variant spellings as regional may ultimately prove valuable. Not all locations for particular manuscripts which have been argued for are included. I have avoided the blanket terms 'south-east' and 'south-west' where other authorities have made such distinctions, but occasionally used 'Kent' when this seemed appropriate. In such cases, the term probably should be seen as meaning the old kingdom of Kent rather than the modern county.

Facsimile references. It is obviously desirable that the reader should be able both to check my decisions on scribal hands and to attempt to link disparate stints in different manuscripts or documents. However, to cite all reproductions of individual manuscript pages is quite beyond the scope of this work. Accordingly, I have confined references in the facsimile column to complete manuscript reproductions, those which are most widely available in permanent form. All of the magnificent EEMF series (cited by volume number), and the less good but certainly useful and inexpensive ASMMF series (cited by volume)[5] are included, plus a number of other generally available books, usually cited by Author-Date. References to facsimiles are confined to the first scribal hand cited for each manuscript.

Contents. Brief reference to the content of manuscripts very often repeats information which may be found in Ker's *Catalogue* or Gneuss and Lapidge's *Anglo-Saxon Manuscripts*, but is intended to help in identifying the material without reference to either of those works. It may also be found useful in showing the distribution of material copied by each scribe in manuscripts worked on by a number of hands, and in identifying the work of hands altering or adding to existing texts.

Notes. This column offers some further information helpful to isolate the hands, or elucidates the contents.

---

[5] Now published by the Arizona Center for Medieval and Renaissance Studies, Tempe, Arizona (Medieval and Renaissance Texts and Studies series).

Abbreviations

ASE	*Anglo-Saxon England*
ASC	*Anglo-Saxon Chronicle*
ASMMF	Anglo-Saxon Manuscripts in Microfiche Facsimile
Barker, 1968	*The York Gospels*, ed. Nicolas Barker, Roxburghe Club (London, 1968)
BL	British Library
CC	Christ Church
Chambers, 1933	*The Exeter Book of Old English Poetry*, with introductory chapters by R. W. Chambers, Max Förster and Robin Flower (Bradford, 1933)
Coll.	College
DC	Dean and Chapter
EEMF	Early English Manuscripts in Facsimile
EETS	Early English Text Society
os	original series
Gneuss	Helmut Gneuss and Michael Lapidge, *Anglo-Saxon Manuscripts* (Toronto, 2014)
Gollancz, 1927	*The Caedmon ms of A-S Biblical Poetry: Junius XI: in the Bodleian Library*, ed. Israel Gollancz (Oxford, 1927)
Kendrick, 1956	T. D. Kendrick, R. L. S. Bruce-Mitford, H. Roosen-Runge, A. S. C. Ross, E. G. Stanley, A. E. A. Warner, *Evangeliorum quattuor Codex Lindisfarnensis*, 2 vols. (Lausanne, 1956–60)
Ker	N. R. Ker, *Catalogue of Manuscripts Containing Anglo-Saxon* (Oxford, 1957)
NM	New Minster
OM	Old Minster
P	David A. E. Pelteret, *Catalogue of English Post-Conquest Vernacular Documents* (Woodbridge, 1990)
StA	St Augustine's
Sawyer or S	P. H. Sawyer, *Anglo-Saxon Charters: An Annotated List and Bibliography*, Royal Historical Society Guides and Handbooks 8 (London, 1968), now supplemented by the electronic Sawyer
Surtees Soc. 136	*Liber Vitae Ecclesiae Dunelmensis*, A collotype facsimile, with an Introduction by A. Hamilton Thompson, Surtees Society vol. 136 (Durham, 1923)
Whitelock, 1968	*The Will of Æthelgifu: A Tenth-Century Anglo-Saxon Manuscript*, ed. Dorothy Whitelock (Oxford, 1968)

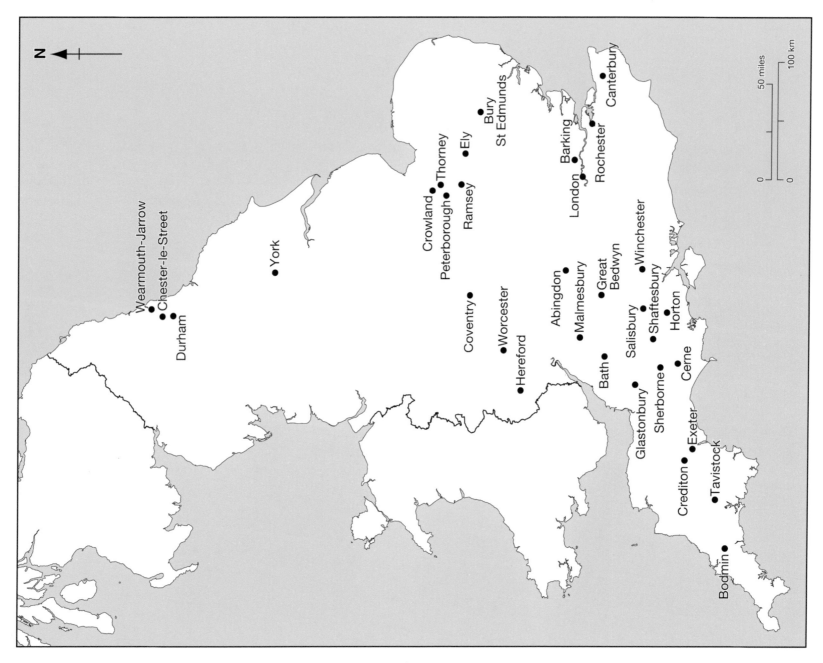

Locations associated with scribal hands

THE CONSPECTUS

HAND NO.	LIBRARY AND SHELF-MARK	GNEUSS	KER	SAWYER/PELTERET	KER HAND NO.	FOLIOS	DATE	LOCATION	FACSIMILE REFERENCES	CONTENTS	NOTES
0.5	Angers, Bibliothèque Municipale 477		App. 40S			96r	X/XI	Brittany	ASMMF 18	scribble	nonsense phrase utilising all OE special characters
1	Antwerp, Plantin-Moretus Museum M 16.2	775	2			$5r^{21}$, $32v^{25}$, $33r^{4}$, $33v^{21}$, $34r^{3}$, $34r^{6}$	X ex. or XI[1]	Abingdon	ASMMF 13	6 glosses to 'Excerptiones de Prisciano'	
1a	Antwerp, Plantin-Moretus Museum M 16.2	775	2			$2r^{14}$, $46r^{13}$	X ex. or XI[1]	Abingdon		2 glosses to 'Excerptiones de Prisciano'	
2	Antwerp, Plantin-Moretus Museum M 16.2 + London, BL, Add. 32246	775	2			Add. 3r–12v	XI in.	Abingdon		7 glosses in Lat.–Lat. glossary, 132 glosses in Lat.–OE glossary	
	Antwerp, Plantin-Moretus Museum M 16.8	776	3			$36r^{7}$			ASMMF 13	2 glosses to Boethius, *De consolatione philosophiae*	
	Brussels, Bibliothèque Royale 1650	806	8	1					ASMMF 13	a few glosses to Aldhelm, *De virginitate*	
3	Antwerp, Plantin-Moretus Museum M 16.2 + London, BL, Add. 32246	775	2			P-M. 3rv, 4r; Add. 2v–7v, 8r, 9r–15r, 17v–21v	XI[1]	Abingdon		glosses in Lat.–OE glossary	
	Brussels, Bibliothèque Royale 1650	806	8	3						many glosses to Aldhelm, *De virginitate*	
4	Antwerp, Plantin-Moretus Museum M 16.2	775	2			$48r^{15,\ 17}$	XI[1]	Abingdon		2 glosses in Latin glossary	
◆	Antwerp, Plantin-Moretus Museum M 16.8, *see Antwerp, Plantin-Moretus Museum M 16.2 + London, BL, Add. 32246*										
4.2	Arras, Bibliothèque Municipale 764, fols. 1–93	779	4			89v, 90r, 93v	X?	Bath?	ASMMF 18	scribbles in margins	
4.3	Arras, Bibliothèque Municipale 764, fols. 134–81	780	5			$164r^{5}$, $168r^{20}$, $174v^{11}$	IX[1] or VIII[2]			1 marginal one-word note and 2 glosses to Isidore, *De ortu et obitu patrum*	
4.5	Berlin, Staatsbibliothek Preussischer Kulturbesitz	792	413				VIII med.			occasional glosses in a Latin glossary	

HAND NO.	LIBRARY AND SHELF-MARK	GNEUSS	KER	SAWYER/PELTERET	KER HAND NO.	FOLIOS	DATE	LOCATION	FACSIMILE REFERENCES	CONTENTS	NOTES
4.6	Bern, Burgerbibliothek 671	794	6	1446a		75v^{1-6}	X^1 or X med.	Great Bedwyn, Wilts	ASMMF 20	tithe notice	
4.7	Bern, Burgerbibliothek 671	794	6			75v^{14}–76r^{12}	X^1 or X med.	Great Bedwyn, Wilts		guild notice	
4.8	Bern, Burgerbibliothek 671	794	6			76v^{1-17}	X^1 or X med.	Great Bedwyn, Wilts		2 manumissions	
◆	Bloomington, Indiana University, Lilly Library, Add. 1000, *see London, BL, Harley 5915, fols. 8–9*										
4.9	Boulogne-sur-Mer, Bibliothèque Municipale 32	799	6*			62r	VIII	Lorsch	ASMMF 18	1 gloss to Ambrose, *De patriarchis*	*hlæs* with *h* superscript
5	Boulogne-sur-Mer, Bibliothèque Municipale 189	805	7		1	4r–11r, 99r, 100r	XI in.	Canterbury CC	ASMMF 18	many glosses to Prudentius anthology	
6	Boulogne-sur-Mer, Bibliothèque Municipale 189	805	7		2	74r–82r	XI in.	Canterbury CC		glosses to Prudentius anthology	
7	Boulogne-sur-Mer, Bibliothèque Municipale 189	805	7		3	100r–104r, 111r–122r, 139r–143r, 190r	XI in.	Canterbury CC		glosses to Prudentius anthology	
8	Boulogne-sur-Mer, Bibliothèque Municipale 189	805	7		4	throughout	XI^1	Canterbury CC		glosses to Prudentius anthology	consonant for vowel cipher
8.1	Boulogne-sur-Mer, Bibliothèque Municipale 189	805	7			44v	XI^1	Canterbury CC		1 gloss	
9	Brussels, Bibliothèque Royale 1650	806	8		2	34r–45r	XI^1	Abingdon	ASMMF 13	fewer than 100 glosses to Aldhelm, *De virginitate*	
10	Brussels, Bibliothèque Royale 1650	806	8		4		XI^1	Abingdon		many glosses to Aldhelm, *De virginitate*	probably more than one hand
◆	Brussels, Bibliothèque Royale 1650, *see Antwerp, Plantin-Moretus Museum M 16.2 + London, BL, Add. 32246*										

HAND NO.	LIBRARY AND SHELF-MARK	GNEUSS	KER	SAWYER/PELTERET	KER HAND NO.	FOLIOS	DATE	LOCATION	FACSIMILE REFERENCES	CONTENTS	NOTES
11	Brussels, Bibliothèque Royale 1828–1830, fols. 36–109	807	9			$50r^{8a}$–$50r^{5c}$	XI in.		ASMMF 13	Lat.–OE glossary	
11a	Brussels, Bibliothèque Royale 1828–1830, fols. 36–109	807	9			$50v^{1a}$–$50v^{23b}$	XI in.			Lat.–OE glossary	
12	Brussels, Bibliothèque Royale 1828–1830, fols. 36–109	807	9			43r, 50v, 51r–68v, 77v, 88v	XI[1]			Lat.–OE glossaries and occasional glosses	
13	Brussels, Bibliothèque Royale 1828–1830, fols. 36–109	807	9			$94r^{9a}$–$95v^{21c}$	XI[1]			Lat.–OE glossaries	
14	Brussels, Bibliothèque Royale 1828–1830, fols. 36–109	807	9			109r	XI			name	*ælfmær*
15	Brussels, Bibliothèque Royale 1828–1830, fols. 36–109	807	9			$109r^{20a}$	XI[1]			1 gloss to a Latin recipe	
15.5	Brussels, Bibliothèque Royale 8558–8563, fols. 1–79	808	10			4r, 16r, 21r, 28r	X[1]		ASMMF 13	6 glosses in margins of Chrodegang, *Regula canonicorum* (enlarged)	
15.7	Brussels, Bibliothèque Royale 8558–8563, fols. 80–131	808	10			$80r^{1-13}$	X	Worcester?		interlinear gloss to *Poenitentiale Pseudo-Theodori*	
16	Brussels, Bibliothèque Royale 8558–8563, fols. 132–153	808	10			132r–139v	XI[1]		ASMMF 13	handbook for a confessor	
17	Brussels, Bibliothèque Royale 8558–8563, fols. 132–153	808	10			$140v$–$153v^{8}$	XI[1]			'Poenitentiale Pseudo-Egberti', Book IV; OE *Canons of Theodore*	
17.5	Brussels, Bibliothèque Royale 8654–8672	App. 6				$202v^{21}$	X?	St Bertin	ASMMF 13		*Godwine fax*
18	Burton-on-Trent Museum, Burton Muniment 1			906, 1536			XI[2] or XI/XII			bounds, will	
19	Burton-on-Trent Museum, Burton Muniment 2			623			XI[1]?			bounds	
20	Burton-on-Trent Museum, Burton Muniment 3			1863		$1r^{10-12}$	XI med.			bounds	fragment
21	Cambridge, Corpus Christi Coll. 9 + BL, Cotton Nero E. i, Pt 1, Pt 2, fols. 1–180, 187–8	36 344	29			Cott. 24r, 27v, 188v–195v; Corp. pp. 23, 24	XI med.	Worcester		glosses to saints' lives	

HAND NO.	LIBRARY AND SHELF-MARK	GNEUSS	KER	SAWYER/PELTERET	KER HAND NO.	FOLIOS	DATE	LOCATION	FACSIMILE REFERENCES	CONTENTS	NOTES
22	Cambridge, Corpus Christi Coll. 9 + BL, Cotton Nero E. i, Pt 1, Pt 2, fols. 1–180, 187–8	36 344	29			Cott. 89rv, 127v–128r, 130r, 147v, 154v; Corp. pp. 218–20, 230–1, 233, 356, 397, 402–3, 405	XI^2	Worcester		directions to readers	
23	Cambridge, Corpus Christi Coll. 12	37	30				X^2	Worcester?	ASMMF 25	Gregory (Alfred), *Regula pastoralis*	
24	Cambridge, Corpus Christi Coll. 23, fols. 1–104	38	31			19r, 34r, 38r, 43r	XI	Malmesbury		7 glosses to Prudentius, *Psychomachia, Peristephanon*	
25	Cambridge, Corpus Christi Coll. 23, fols. 1–104	38	31	1		1v–19r	X/XI	Canterbury or Malmesbury?		translations of titles to illustrations 1–8, 10–44	
26	Cambridge, Corpus Christi Coll. 23, fols. 1–104	38	31	2		19v–21v	XI med.	Malmesbury		translations of titles to illustrations 45–8	
27	Cambridge, Corpus Christi Coll. 23, fols. 1–104	38	31	3		24v, 29r, 33v	XI^2 or XI/XII	Malmesbury		translations of titles to illustrations 57, 66, 78	
28	Cambridge, Corpus Christi Coll. 41	39	32	1		pp. 1–190^{20}	XI^1		ASMMF 11	OE Bede	
29	Cambridge, Corpus Christi Coll. 41	39	32	2		pp. 190–488	XI^1			OE Bede	
30	Cambridge, Corpus Christi Coll. 41	39	32			pp. 155, 242	XI^1			names	*ælfwine, ælfwerd*
31	Cambridge, Corpus Christi Coll. 41	39	32			pp. 122–32, 182, 196–8, 206, 208, 254–301, 326, 350–3, 402–17, 484–8	XI^1 or XI med.			charms, homilies, martyrology (part), verse dialogue and rubrics to liturgy, all in margins	
32	Cambridge, Corpus Christi Coll. 41	39	32	P 92		p. 488	XI^2	Exeter		Leofric ascription	
33	Cambridge, Corpus Christi Coll. 44	40	33			1r–2r	XI	Canterbury		end of Amalarius, *Liber officialis* III.i	partly lost and erased, except for note on church bells
34	Cambridge, Corpus Christi Coll. 44	40	33			53v, 65v, 66v	XI	Canterbury		4 glosses in a pontifical	
35	Cambridge, Corpus Christi Coll. 57	41	34			3r^{23}, 5r^7, 5v^7, 10v^{20}, 18r^{24}	XI^1	Abingdon or Canterbury	ASMMF 11	5 glosses to Benedictine Rule	
36	Cambridge, Corpus Christi Coll. 57	41	34			7r^{27}, 9r^{11}	XI^1	Abingdon or Canterbury		2 more glosses	

HAND NO.	LIBRARY AND SHELF-MARK	GNEUSS	KER	SAWYER/PELTERET	KER HAND NO.	FOLIOS	DATE	LOCATION	FACSIMILE REFERENCES	CONTENTS	NOTES
37	Cambridge, Corpus Christi Coll. 57	41	34			$8r^{11}$, $8r^{15}$	XI med.	Abingdon or Canterbury		2 more glosses	
38	Cambridge, Corpus Christi Coll. 57	41	34			$7v^{10}$	XI med.	Abingdon or Canterbury		1 more gloss	
39	Cambridge, Corpus Christi Coll. 57	41	34			$23v^{2}$	XI^{1}	Abingdon or Canterbury		1 more gloss in margin	
40	Cambridge, Corpus Christi Coll. 111, pp. 7, 8, 55–6 + Cambridge, Corpus Christi Coll. 140	44	35	P 70–2		III. p. 7^{1-27}	XI^{2}	Bath		lists of relics	
41	Cambridge, Corpus Christi Coll. 111, pp. 7, 8, 55–6 + Cambridge, Corpus Christi Coll. 140	44	35	P 73–6 P 78 P 81		III. p. 8^{1-24} III. p. 56^{27} 140. $1r^{6-8}$ 140. $71r$–$72v$	XI^{2}	Bath		4 manumissions 7-word final addition to agreement (see below) manumission Sunday letter homily	
42	Cambridge, Corpus Christi Coll. 111, pp. 7, 8, 55–6 + Cambridge, Corpus Christi Coll. 140	44	35	P 77		III. p. 8^{25-7}	XI^{2}	Bath		manumission	
43	Cambridge, Corpus Christi Coll. 111, pp. 7, 8, 55–6 + Cambridge, Corpus Christi Coll. 140	44	35	P 78		III. pp. 55–6	XI^{2}	Bath		agreement	
44	Cambridge, Corpus Christi Coll. 111, pp. 7, 8, 55–6 + Cambridge, Corpus Christi Coll. 140	44	35	P 78		III. p. 56^{26-7}	XI^{2}	Bath		penultimate addition to agreement	
45	Cambridge, Corpus Christi Coll. 140	44	35	P 79		$1r^{1-3}$	XI^{2}	Bath		manumission	
46	Cambridge, Corpus Christi Coll. 140	44	35	P 80		$1r^{4-6}$	XI^{2}	Bath		manumission	
47	Cambridge, Corpus Christi Coll. 140	44	35	P 82		$1r^{9-12}$	XI/XII	Bath		manumission	
48	Cambridge, Corpus Christi Coll. 140	44	35	P 83		$1v^{1-4}$	XI/XII	Bath		manumission	
49	Cambridge, Corpus Christi Coll. 140	44	35	P 84		$1v^{5-6}$	XI^{2}	Bath		manumission	
50	Cambridge, Corpus Christi Coll. 140	44	35	P 85		$1v^{7-9}$	XI/XII	Bath		manumission	
51	Cambridge, Corpus Christi Coll. 140	44	35			$1v^{15-22}$	XI med./XI^{2}	Bath		3 manumissions	

HAND NO.	LIBRARY AND SHELF-MARK	GNEUSS	KER	SAWYER/PELTERET	KER HAND NO.	FOLIOS	DATE	LOCATION	FACSIMILE REFERENCES	CONTENTS	NOTES
52	Cambridge, Corpus Christi Coll. 140	44	35			$2r–45v^4$	XI^1	Bath		Gospels: Matthew	scribe: Ælfric of Bath name: *brihtwold*
53	Cambridge, Corpus Christi Coll. 140	44	35			$46r–58r^{25}$, $58v^1–71r^{12}$	XI^1	Bath		Mark	
54	Cambridge, Corpus Christi Coll. 140	44	35			$58r^{26–38}$, $73r–114r$	XI^1	Bath		Luke and Mark 12:26–38	
55	Cambridge, Corpus Christi Coll. 140	44	35			$116r^1–147r^{15}$	XI^1	Bath		John	
55.3	Cambridge, Corpus Christi Coll. 144	45	36			1r–61rv	IX^1		ASMMF 25	2 glossaries	2nd: 'Corpus Glossary'
55.4	Cambridge, Corpus Christi Coll. 144	45	36			i r	X^2			additions in Latin and OE	
55.5	Cambridge, Corpus Christi Coll. 144	45	36			ii r	X/XI			3 glosses	
56	Cambridge, Corpus Christi Coll. 146	46	37			pp. 303–4, 308–9	XI in.			adjurations	
57	Cambridge, Corpus Christi Coll. 162, pp. 1–138, 161–564	50	38			pp. 1–563	X/XI	Canterbury StA	ASMMF 25	homilies	main scribe
58	Cambridge, Corpus Christi Coll. 162, pp. 1–138, 161–564	50	38			p. $563^{9–23}$	XI in.	Canterbury StA		beginning of a homily on Augustine of Canterbury	early addition
59	Cambridge, Corpus Christi Coll. 162, pp. 1–138, 161–564	50	38			pp. 39, 40, 43	XI in.	Canterbury StA		added text	head and foot
60	Cambridge, Corpus Christi Coll. 162, pp. 1–138, 161–564	50	38			pp. 174, 198	XI in.	Canterbury StA		additions	
60a	Cambridge, Corpus Christi Coll. 162, pp. 1–138, 161–564	50	38			pp. 107, 423	XI in.	Canterbury StA		additions	
60.5	Cambridge, Corpus Christi Coll. 162, pp. 1–138, 161–564	50	38			p. 243	XI in.	Canterbury StA		added text	
61	Cambridge, Corpus Christi Coll. 162, pp. 1–138, 161–564	50	38			pp. 288, 289	XI med.	Canterbury StA		extensive marginal additions	
61.5	Cambridge, Corpus Christi Coll. 162, pp. 1–138, 161–564	50	38			p. 412	XI med.	Canterbury StA		marginal addition	
62	Cambridge, Corpus Christi Coll. 162, pp. 1–138, 161–564	50	38			pp. 322–33	XI	Canterbury StA		textual alterations to one item	

HAND NO.	LIBRARY AND SHELF-MARK	GNEUSS	KER	SAWYER/ÞELTERET	KER HAND NO.	FOLIOS	DATE	LOCATION	FACSIMILE REFERENCES	CONTENTS	NOTES
63	Cambridge, Corpus Christi Coll. 162, pp. 1–138, 161–564	50	38			pp. 161–75, 478–82	XI in.	Canterbury StA		alterations here and frequently in minor changes elsewhere	
64	Cambridge, Corpus Christi Coll. 162, pp. 1–138, 161–564	50	38			pp. 403–31	XI in.	Canterbury StA		extensive alterations and additions here and occasionally in successive items	
65	Cambridge, Corpus Christi Coll. 162, pp. 1–138, 161–564	50	38			e.g. p. 10^9	XI in.	Canterbury StA		frequent minor alterations throughout	
65.5	Cambridge, Corpus Christi Coll. 162, pp. 1–138, 161–564	50	38			p. 219^{1,7}	XI in.	Canterbury StA		minor additions in black writing	
66	Cambridge, Corpus Christi Coll. 162, pp. 1–138, 161–564	50	38			e.g. pp. 11^1, 13^9	XI in.	Canterbury StA		minor additions in pale writing	
66.5	Cambridge, Corpus Christi Coll. 162, pp. 1–138, 161–564	50	38			pp. 365–82	XI^2	Canterbury StA		extensive alterations to one item	
67	Cambridge, Corpus Christi Coll. 162, pp. 1–138, 161–564	50	38			e.g. p. 404	XI^2	Canterbury StA		occasional alterations	
68	Cambridge, Corpus Christi Coll. 162, pp. 1–138, 161–564	50	38			e.g. p. 406	XI^2	Canterbury StA		occasional alterations in a fine hand	
69	Cambridge, Corpus Christi Coll. 162, pp. 1–138, 161–564	50	38			pp. 293–4	XI	Canterbury StA		directions to readers	
◆	Cambridge, Corpus Christi Coll. 162, pp. 139–60, *see Cambridge, Corpus Christi Coll. 178*										
69.1	Cambridge, Corpus Christi Coll. 173, fols. 1–56	52	39		1	1r–12v^{22}, 12v^{26}–16r	IX/X	Winchester OM?	EETS 208	*ASC* A: annals 1–891	
69.1a	Cambridge, Corpus Christi Coll. 173, fols. 1–56	52	39			12v$^{23–24}$					duplicate material, now erased but legible
69.1b	Cambridge, Corpus Christi Coll. 173, fols. 1–56	52	39			13v					top margin: entry of material originally written by main scribe and later erased

HAND NO.	LIBRARY AND SHELF-MARK	GNEUSS	KER	SAWYER/PELTERET	KER HAND NO.	FOLIOS	DATE	LOCATION	FACSIMILE REFERENCES	CONTENTS	NOTES
69.2	Cambridge, Corpus Christi Coll. 173, fols. 1–56	52	39		2	$16v–21v^{21}$	X¹ or X med.			annals 891–924	
	London, BL, Add. 47967	300	133						EEMF 3	Orosius, *Historiae adversum paganos*	
69.2a	Cambridge, Corpus Christi Coll. 173, fols. 1–56	52	39			$25r^{1–7}$					perhaps uncertain writing by Ker's scribe 2
69.3	Cambridge, Corpus Christi Coll. 173, fols. 1–56	52	39			$21r^{22}–23v^{12}$, $23v^{16}–24v^{21}$, $25r^{8}–25v$					
69.4	Cambridge, Corpus Christi Coll. 173, fols. 1–56	52	39			$23v^{12–15}$					
69.5	Cambridge, Corpus Christi Coll. 173, fols. 1–56	52	39			$24v^{22–25}$					
69.6	Cambridge, Corpus Christi Coll. 173, fols. 1–56	52	39		3	$26v–27v^{17}$	X med.	Winchester?		annals 925–55	
	London, BL, Cotton Otho B. xi + Cotton Otho B. x, fols. 55, 58, 62	357	180		1	B.xi, $1r–34v$, $37r–38v$; B.x, $55rv$, $58rv$, $62rv$				Bede, *Ecclesiastical History*	
	London, BL, Royal 12 D. XVII	479	264			$1r–127v$			EEMF 5, ASMMF 1	medical recipes in 3 collections	name *Bald* in Latin colophon to 2nd collection
69.7	Cambridge, Corpus Christi Coll. 173, fols. 1–56	52	39			$27v^{20–21}$	X med.			annal for 951	
69.7a	London, BL, Cotton Charter viii. 12			636						bounds	
70	Cambridge, Corpus Christi Coll. 173, fols. 1–56	52	39		4	$28r^{3–25}$	X²	Winchester?	EETS os 208	annals 962–4	
71	Cambridge, Corpus Christi Coll. 173, fols. 1–56	52	39		5	$28v^{6}–30r^{14}$	XI in.	Winchester?		annals 973–1001	
72	Cambridge, Corpus Christi Coll. 173, fols. 1–56	52	39			$30r^{14–15}$	XI¹ (1001 × 1013)	Winchester?		11 words added to annal 1001	
72.5	Cambridge, Corpus Christi Coll. 173, fols. 1–56	52	39		6	$33r–35r^{18}$, $36r–52v^{19}$	X med.			table of chapters; laws of Alfred and Ine	

HAND NO.	LIBRARY AND SHELF-MARK	GNEUSS	KER	SAWYER/PELTERET	KER HAND NO.	FOLIOS	DATE	LOCATION	FACSIMILE REFERENCES	CONTENTS	NOTES
73	Cambridge, Corpus Christi Coll. 173, fols. 1–56	52	39			$8v^{19-21}$	?XI¹ (before 1013)	Winchester?		marginal addition to annal 688, cf. also insertion in annal 728 ($9v^4$)	
74	Cambridge, Corpus Christi Coll. 173, fols. 1–56	52	39			$20r^{21}$	XI¹			addition in annal 902	date of Grimbold's death
75	Cambridge, Corpus Christi Coll. 173, fols. 1–56	52	39			$3ra^{14}$, $3vb^2$	XI¹			additions to annals 200 and 300	
76	Cambridge, Corpus Christi Coll. 173, fols. 1–56	52	39			$31v^{19-26}$	XI² or XI/XII	Canterbury CC		additions incl. annal for 1070	
77	Cambridge, Corpus Christi Coll. 173, fols. 1–56	52	39			$13v^{32}$, $16r^{25}$				additions to annals 870 and 890	
78	Cambridge, Corpus Christi Coll. 173, fols. 1–56	52	39				XI/XII	Canterbury CC		additions to annals up to 616	
	London, BL, Campbell Charter xxi, 5			1088		$1r^{4-10}$				alterations to writ	
	Canterbury, Cathedral Library, Chart. Ant. C. 4			P 22						alterations to writ	
	London, BL, Cotton Domitian viii	328	148			30r–65v, $66r^{14}$–70v				Chronicle F	
78a	Cambridge, Corpus Christi Coll. 173, fols. 1–56	52	39			$1va^{16}$	XI/XII	Canterbury CC		annal 11	
78b	Cambridge, Corpus Christi Coll. 173, fols. 1–56	52	39			$7v^{14-15}$, $9v^{1-2}$, $9v^{34}$	XI/XII	Canterbury CC		additions to annals 640, 725 and 748	also bottom margin of 7v
78c	Cambridge, Corpus Christi Coll. 173, fols. 1–56	52	39			$10v^{20, 28}$	XI/XII	Canterbury CC		additions to annal 760	
78d	Cambridge, Corpus Christi Coll. 173, fols. 1–56	52	39			$11r^{11}$	XI/XII	Canterbury CC		addition to annal 784	
78e	Cambridge, Corpus Christi Coll. 173, fols. 1–56	52	39			$26r^{2-3}$	XI/XII	Canterbury CC		addition to annal 924	
78f	Cambridge, Corpus Christi Coll. 173, fols. 1–56	52	39			$27r^{16-17}$	XI/XII	Canterbury CC		addition to annal 940	

HAND NO.	LIBRARY AND SHELF-MARK	GNEUSS	KER	SAWYER/PELTERET	KER HAND NO.	FOLIOS	DATE	LOCATION	FACSIMILE REFERENCES	CONTENTS	NOTES
78g	Cambridge, Corpus Christi Coll. 173, fols. 1–56	52	39			31r^{2-6}, 31v^{23}–32r^{12}	XI/XII	Canterbury CC		additions to annals 1031 and 1070	
79	Cambridge, Corpus Christi Coll. 173, fols. 1–56	52	39			5v^{30-1}	XI/XII	Canterbury CC		addition on palimpsest in annal 519	
80	Cambridge, Corpus Christi Coll. 173, fols. 1–56	52	39			30r^{24}–31v^{13}	XI/XII	Canterbury CC		annals 1005–1067	
80a	Cambridge, Corpus Christi Coll. 173, fols. 1–56	52	39			25r^{23}	XI/XII	Canterbury CC		additions to annal 919	
81	Cambridge, Corpus Christi Coll. 173, fols. 1–56	52	39			31v^{13-16}	XI/XII	Canterbury CC		addition to annal 1066	
82	Cambridge, Corpus Christi Coll. 173, fols. 57–83	53	40				X/XI	Winchester?		glosses to Sedulius, *Carmen paschale*, 2 hymns	
83	Cambridge, Corpus Christi Coll. 178, Part A, + Cambridge, Corpus Christi Coll. 162, pp. 139–60	54	41	1		178. pp. 1^1–169^{30}; 162. pp. 139–60	XI^1	Worcester?	ASMMF 25	homilies	
84	Cambridge, Corpus Christi Coll. 178, Part A	54	41	2		pp. 170^1–270^{30}	XI^1	Worcester?		homilies (cont.)	
85	Cambridge, Corpus Christi Coll. 178, Part A	54	41				XI med.	Worcester?		frequent alterations throughout	
86	Cambridge, Corpus Christi Coll. 178, Part A	54	41			pp. 253–7	XI med.	Worcester?		further alterations	
87	Cambridge, Corpus Christi Coll. 178, Part A, + Cambridge, Corpus Christi Coll. 162, pp. 139–60	54	41			178. pp. 119, 120, 124, 229; 162. p. 142	XI ex.	Worcester		marginal additions	scribe: Coleman
	Cambridge, Corpus Christi Coll. 265	73	53			pp. 41, 74–5, 77–8					
	Cambridge, University Library Kk. 3. 18	22	23			84r, 85r, 87v					
	Oxford, Bodleian Lib., Hatton 113 + 114	637 638	331			Hatt. 113. 70v, 78rv, 108v, 128v, 134r; Hatt. 114. 11v, 13v, 25r, 86r^8, 90v^9, 113r^8					
	Oxford, Bodleian Library, Junius 121	644	338			28$v^{4,6}$, 51v, 82v^6?					

HAND NO.	LIBRARY AND SHELF-MARK	GNEUSS	KER	SAWYER/PELTERET	KER HAND NO.	FOLIOS	DATE	LOCATION	FACSIMILE REFERENCES	CONTENTS	NOTES
88	Cambridge, Corpus Christi Coll. 178, Part A	54	41			pp. 254, 255	XI²	Worcester		additions in margins	
89	Cambridge, Corpus Christi Coll. 178, Part B	55	41			pp. 287¹–457²²	XI¹	Worcester?		Benedictine Rule	
90	Cambridge, Corpus Christi Coll. 178, Part B	55	41			pp. 416, 425	XI²	Worcester		alterations	
91	Cambridge, Corpus Christi Coll. 178, Part B	55	41			p. 458¹⁻¹⁰	XI²	Worcester		homiletic fragment	
91.7	Cambridge, Corpus Christi Coll. 183	56	42			70r	X¹			19 glosses in glossary of Bede, *Vita S.Cuthberti* (verse)	
91.9	Cambridge, Corpus Christi Coll. 183	56	42			96v	X			list of ecclesiastical vessels	
92	Cambridge, Corpus Christi Coll. 183	56	42	P 61		96v²³⁻⁶	1071 × 1080	Durham		land memorandum	
93	Cambridge, Corpus Christi Coll. 188	58	43				XI¹	Hereford?		homilies	
94	Cambridge, Corpus Christi Coll. 188	58	43			p. 61	XI²	Hereford?		name	*sawulf*
95	Cambridge, Corpus Christi Coll. 190, fols. 1–294	59	45			p. 17	1050 × 1072	Exeter		gloss to *Excerptiones Pseudo-Egberti*	in margin
96	Cambridge, Corpus Christi Coll. 190, fols. 1–294	59	45			p. 130¹⁸⁻²¹	XI med.	Exeter		charm	
97	Cambridge, Corpus Christi Coll. 190, pp. 1–294	59	45			p. 246	XI¹			glosses to antiphon	
98	Cambridge, Corpus Christi Coll. 190, pp. 1–294	59	45			p. 265–6	XI¹			glosses to Defensor of Ligugé, *Liber scintillarum*	
99	Cambridge, Corpus Christi Coll. 190, pp. 295–420	59.5	45			pp. 295¹–308	XI²	Exeter		pastoral letter	
100	Cambridge, Corpus Christi Coll. 190, pp. 295–420	59.5	45			pp. 308–19²⁸	XI²	Exeter		homily; *De ecclesiasticis gradibus*	
101	Cambridge, Corpus Christi Coll. 190, pp. 295–420	59.5	45			pp. 320¹⁵–350²⁸	XI²	Exeter		pastoral letters	
102	Cambridge, Corpus Christi Coll. 190, pp. 295–420	59.5	45			pp. 351¹–359¹³	XI²	Exeter		homilies	

HAND NO.	LIBRARY AND SHELF-MARK	GNEUSS	KER	SAWYER/PELTERET	KER HAND NO.	FOLIOS	DATE	LOCATION	FACSIMILE REFERENCES	CONTENTS	NOTES
103	Cambridge, Corpus Christi Coll. 190, pp. 295–420	59.5	45			p. 365$^{1-25}$	XI^2	Exeter		form of confession	
104	Cambridge, Corpus Christi Coll. 190, pp. 295–420	59.5	45			pp. 366^1–418^{15}	XI med.			penitentials	
105	Cambridge, Corpus Christi Coll. 190, pp. 295–420	59.5	45			pp. 418^{16}–420^4	XI^2			laws	
106	Cambridge, Corpus Christi Coll. 191	60	46				1050 × 1072	Exeter	ASMMF 11	Chrodegang, *Regula canonicorum*	main hand
	Cambridge, Corpus Christi Coll. 201, pp. 179–272	66	50			pp. 179–269^6				Theodulf of Orleans, *Capitula*, homily	
	Cambridge, Corpus Christi Coll. 421	109	69			pp. 3–93				homilies	
	London, BL, Cotton Cleopatra B. xiii, fols. 1–58	322	144		4	38r^4–55v^{13}				homilies	
	Oxford, Bodleian Library Auct. F. 1. 15, fols. 1–77	533	294	P 92		77v				Leofric ascription	
106a	Cambridge, Corpus Christi Coll. 191	60	46				1050 × 1072	Exeter			possible second hand
107	Cambridge, Corpus Christi Coll. 191	60	46			e.g. pp. 19, 20, 128, 155	1050 × 1072	Exeter		frequent minor corrections	
108	Cambridge, Corpus Christi Coll. 191	60	46			e.g. pp. 33, 48, 134, 157	1050 × 1072	Exeter		glosses	
109	Cambridge, Corpus Christi Coll. 196	62	47			pp. 1–110	1050 × 1072	Exeter		martyrology fragment	
110	Cambridge, Corpus Christi Coll. 196	62	47			pp. 111–22	1050 × 1072	Exeter		*Vindicta salvatoris*	
111	Cambridge, Corpus Christi Coll. 198	64	48		1	1r–23v^{26}	XI^1			homilies	
112	Cambridge, Corpus Christi Coll. 198	64	48		2	24r^1–87v^{26}, 160r^1–201v^{26}	XI^1			homilies	
113	Cambridge, Corpus Christi Coll. 198	64	48		3	88r^1–149v^{26}, 202r^1–217v^{15}	XI^1			homilies	
114	Cambridge, Corpus Christi Coll. 198	64	48		4	248r^1–287v^{26}	XI^1			homilies	

HAND NO.	LIBRARY AND SHELF-MARK	GNEUSS	KER	SAWYER/PELTERET	KER HAND NO.	FOLIOS	DATE	LOCATION	FACSIMILE REFERENCES	CONTENTS	NOTES
115	Cambridge, Corpus Christi Coll. 198	64	48	5	$150r^1$–$9v^{18}$, $218r^1$–$245r^{11}$	XI[1]				
115a	Cambridge, Corpus Christi Coll. 198	64	48	5a	$245r^{12}$–$247v^{23}$	XI[1]				homilies	
116	Cambridge, Corpus Christi Coll. 198	64	48	6	$328r^1$–$350r^6$, $360r^1$–$366v^{25}$, $378r^1$–$385v^{25}$	XI[1]				homilies	
116a	Cambridge, Corpus Christi Coll. 198	64	48	7a	$366v$	XI[1]				homily (cont.)	
117	Cambridge, Corpus Christi Coll. 198	64	48	7	$350r^8$–$359r^{15}$	XI[1]				homilies	
118	Cambridge, Corpus Christi Coll. 198	64	48	8	$288r^1$–$321r^{22}$, $386r^1$–$394v^{19}$	XI[1]				homilies	
119	Cambridge, Corpus Christi Coll. 198	64	48	9	$321v^{1-26}$, $367r^1$–$374v^8$	XI[2]	Worcester?		added homilies	
120	Cambridge, Corpus Christi Coll. 198	64	48	10	$322r^1$–$327v^{27}$	XI[2]	Worcester?		added homilies	
121	Cambridge, Corpus Christi Coll. 198	64	48		$322r^{18}$	XI				*blacc* in margin against *blæc*
122	Cambridge, Corpus Christi Coll. 198	64	48	11	$374v^{11}$–$377r^6$	XI[2]	Worcester?		added homilies	
123	Cambridge, Corpus Christi Coll. 198	64	48		$323v$	XI			name	*æðelric*
124	Cambridge, Corpus Christi Coll. 198	64	48		$321r^{25-6}$	XI[2]	Worcester?		charter?	palimpsest fragment; name: *ulf*
125	Cambridge, Corpus Christi Coll. 201, pp. 1–178	65	49		pp. 1–7, 161–167^8	XI in.			*Regularis concordia*, OE verse	
126	Cambridge, Corpus Christi Coll. 201, pp. 1–178	65	49		p. 161	XI			alteration	
126a	Cambridge, Corpus Christi Coll. 201, pp. 1–178	65	49		p. 166	XI			alteration	
127	Cambridge, Corpus Christi Coll. 201, pp. 1–178	65.5	49		pp. 8–151^3, 167^{11}–170^8	XI med.	Winchester NM?		homilies, laws, *Apollonius of Tyre*, resting places of saints, verse	
127.5	Cambridge, Corpus Christi Coll. 201	65.5	49			XI?			pagination in green	quires 2–6, except first and last pages of each quire; bottom margin

HAND NO.	LIBRARY AND SHELF-MARK	GNEUSS	KER	SAWYER/PELTERET	KER HAND NO.	FOLIOS	DATE	LOCATION	FACSIMILE REFERENCES	CONTENTS	NOTES
128	Cambridge, Corpus Christi Coll. 201, pp. 1–178	65.5	49			pp. 151⁴–160	XI med.	Winchester NM?		Genesis	
129	Cambridge, Corpus Christi Coll. 201, pp. 1–178	65.5	49			p. 29	XI med.	Winchester NM?		alteration	
130	Cambridge, Corpus Christi Coll. 201, pp. 1–178	65.5	49			p. 32	XI	Winchester NM?		alteration	
131	Cambridge, Corpus Christi Coll. 201, pp. 1–178	65.5	49			p. 47	XI	Winchester NM?		alteration	
132	Cambridge, Corpus Christi Coll. 201, pp. 1–178	65.5	49			p. 73	XI	Winchester NM?		alteration	
133	Cambridge, Corpus Christi Coll. 201, pp. 1–178	65.5	49			p. 98	XI	Winchester NM?		alteration	
134	Cambridge, Corpus Christi Coll. 201, pp. 1–178	65.5	49			p. 111	XI	Winchester NM?		alteration	
135	Cambridge, Corpus Christi Coll. 201, pp. 1–178	65.5	49			p. 121	XI	Winchester NM?		alteration	
136	Cambridge, Corpus Christi Coll. 201, pp. 1–178	65.5	49			p. 131	XI	Winchester NM?		marginal addition	
137	Cambridge, Corpus Christi Coll. 201, pp. 1–178	65.5	49			p. 134	XI	Winchester NM?		alteration	
◆	Cambridge, Corpus Christi Coll. 201, pp. 179–272, *see Cambridge, Corpus Christi Coll. 191*										
138	Cambridge, Corpus Christi Coll. 214	68	51				XI¹			continuous gloss to Boethius, *De consolatione philosophiæ*	main hand
139	Cambridge, Corpus Christi Coll. 214	68	51			36r–39r, 68rv	XI¹			additional glosses	
140	Cambridge, Corpus Christi Coll. 223	70	52			pp. 11, 13, 18, 42	XI¹			glosses to Prudentius anthology	
141	Cambridge, Corpus Christi Coll. 223	70	52			p. 2	X or XI			glosses to names of herbs	
142	Cambridge, Corpus Christi Coll. 265	73	53			pp. 72²³–83²¹	XI med.	Worcester		directions for a confessor	

HAND NO.	LIBRARY AND SHELF-MARK	GNEUSS	KER	SAWYER/PELTERET	KER HAND NO.	FOLIOS	DATE	LOCATION	FACSIMILE REFERENCES	CONTENTS	NOTES
143	Cambridge, Corpus Christi Coll. 265	73	53			pp. 222⁶–224¹⁹, 225¹³–227²⁴	XI med.	Worcester		law code	
144	Cambridge, Corpus Christi Coll. 265	73	53			pp. 224²⁰–225¹²	XI med.	Worcester		laws	
♦	Cambridge, Corpus Christi Coll. 265, *see Cambridge, Corpus Christi Coll. 178, Part A*										
145	Cambridge, Corpus Christi Coll. 265	73	53			pp. 30, 39	XI²	Worcester		2 glosses to canon law and *Poenitentiale Egberti*	
146	Cambridge, Corpus Christi Coll. 265	73	53			p. 54	XI²	Worcester		glosses to *Poenitentiale Pseudo-Theodori*	
147	Cambridge, Corpus Christi Coll. 265	73	53			p. 60	XI²	Worcester		1 gloss to *Poenitentiale Pseudo-Theodori*	
148	Cambridge, Corpus Christi Coll. 265	73	53			p. 61	XI²	Worcester		1 gloss to capitulary excerpt	
149	Cambridge, Corpus Christi Coll. 265	73	53			p. 63	XI²	Worcester		glosses to capitulary excerpt	
150	Cambridge, Corpus Christi Coll. 265	73	53			p. 112	XI²	Worcester		6 names of relationship in Latin and English	in margin
151	Cambridge, Corpus Christi Coll. 265	73	53			p. 122	XI²	Worcester		1 gloss to Theodulf of Orleans, *Capitula*	
152	Cambridge, Corpus Christi Coll. 265	73	53			p. 136	XI²	Worcester		2 glosses to Theodulf of Orleans, *Capitula*	
153	Cambridge, Corpus Christi Coll. 285, fols. 75–131	82	54			84r, 117r, 126r, 129r	XI¹			5 glosses to Aldhelm, *Carmen de virginitate*	
154	Cambridge, Corpus Christi Coll. 285	82	54			110v	XI¹			1 additional gloss	
155	Cambridge, Corpus Christi Coll. 286	83	55	1455		77v¹⁻¹¹	989–1006	Canterbury StA		record in English	
156	Cambridge, Corpus Christi Coll. 286	83	55			2r	989–1006	Canterbury StA		names	in margin: *siferð, tate*
156.5	Cambridge, Corpus Christi Coll. 286	83	55	1198		74v¹⁻²⁰	X¹	Canterbury StA		grant	

HAND NO.	LIBRARY AND SHELF-MARK	GNEUSS	KER	SAWYER/PELTERET	KER HAND NO.	FOLIOS	DATE	LOCATION	FACSIMILE REFERENCES	CONTENTS	NOTES
157	Cambridge, Corpus Christi Coll. 302	86	56				XI/XII		ASMMF 11	homilies	main hand
158	Cambridge, Corpus Christi Coll. 302	86	56			p. 29$^{1-8}$	XI/XII			homily (part)	intervening hand
159	Cambridge, Corpus Christi Coll. 320, fols. 117–70	90	58			117rv, 170r	X/XI	Canterbury StA		confessional texts	
160	Cambridge, Corpus Christi Coll. 321	91	59			139*r	XI^1 or XI med.			dialogue fragment	
161	Cambridge, Corpus Christi Coll. 322	92	60				XI^2			Gregory, *Dialogi*	
162	Cambridge, Corpus Christi Coll. 326	93	61			pp. 5–6	X^2	Canterbury CC	ASMMF 25	macaronic verse	
163	Cambridge, Corpus Christi Coll. 326	93	61	b			X^2	Canterbury CC		66 glosses to Aldhelm, *De virginitate*	
164	Cambridge, Corpus Christi Coll. 326	93	61	b			XI in.	Canterbury CC		27 further glosses	
165	Cambridge, Corpus Christi Coll. 326	93	61			p. 139	XI in.	Canterbury CC		single word	*fotgewædu*
166	Cambridge, Corpus Christi Coll. 367, Pt II	100	64	a		48v^{2-4}	XI med.	Worcester?		booklist	
167	Cambridge, Corpus Christi Coll. 367, Pt II	100	64	b		48v^5–50v	XI^2	Worcester?		Vision of Leofric	
168	Cambridge, Corpus Christi Coll. 383	102	65			pp. 1–107^{14}	XI/XII	London, St Paul's		laws	
169	Cambridge, Corpus Christi Coll. 383	102	65				XI/XII	London, St Paul's		corrections and alterations	
170	Cambridge, Corpus Christi Coll. 389	103	66				X^2	Canterbury StA		glosses to Felix, *St Guthlac*	
171	Cambridge, Corpus Christi Coll. 391	104	67	I		pp. 613–17, 713–21	XI^2	Worcester		prayers, prognostics	

HAND NO.	LIBRARY AND SHELF-MARK	GNEUSS	KER	SAWYER/PELTERET	KER HAND NO.	FOLIOS	DATE	LOCATION	FACSIMILE REFERENCES	CONTENTS	NOTES
172	Cambridge, Corpus Christi Coll. 391	104	67		2	pp. 601–3, 611–12	XI^2	Worcester		prayers	scribe: Hemming
	Cambridge, University Library Kk. 3. 18	22	23							OE Bede	
	London, BL, Harley Charter 83. A. 3			1421						charter in English	
	London, BL, Cotton Tiberius A. xiii	366	190	P146–7		177r, 180v–181v, 190r				cartulary	for charters, see Sawyer, pp. 52–3
	Oxford, Bodleian Library, Hatton 114	638	331		5	$246v^{2-23}$			ASMMF 6	homily	
	Oxford, Bodleian Library, Junius 121	644	338		3	$148v^{10-22}$, 150r, $150v^{16}$–151r, 152r–153v, $154r^{17}$–$154v^{12}$			ASMMF 6	homily	
173	Cambridge, Corpus Christi Coll. 391	104	67		3	pp. 617–18	XI/XII	Worcester		addresses to the cross	
174	Cambridge, Corpus Christi Coll. 419	108	68			pp. 1–366	XI^1		ASMMF 8	homilies	
	Cambridge, Corpus Christi Coll. 421	109	69			pp. 99–108, 227–354			ASMMF 8		
175	Cambridge, Corpus Christi Coll. 421	109	69			p. 2^{1-17}	XI^1			invitation to prayer	
176	Cambridge, Corpus Christi Coll. 419	108	68				XI^1			corrections	
	Cambridge, Corpus Christi Coll. 421	109	69								
176a	Cambridge, Corpus Christi Coll. 419	108	68				XI^1			further corrections	
	Cambridge, Corpus Christi Coll. 421	109	69								
176b	Cambridge, Corpus Christi Coll. 419	108	68				XI^1			further corrections	
	Cambridge, Corpus Christi Coll. 421	109	69								
176c	Cambridge, Corpus Christi Coll. 419	108	68				XI^1			further corrections	
	Cambridge, Corpus Christi Coll. 421	109	69								
176d	Cambridge, Corpus Christi Coll. 419	108	68				XI^1			further corrections	
	Cambridge, Corpus Christi Coll. 421	109	69								
◆	Cambridge, Corpus Christi Coll. 421, *see Cambridge, Corpus Christi Coll. 191*										

HAND NO.	LIBRARY AND SHELF-MARK	GNEUSS	KER	SAWYER/PELTERET	KER HAND NO.	FOLIOS	DATE	LOCATION	FACSIMILE REFERENCES	CONTENTS	NOTES
177	Cambridge, Corpus Christi Coll. 421	109	69			pp. 94–6	XI²	Exeter		homilies	
178	Cambridge, Corpus Christi Coll. 421	109	69			pp. 209–24	XI²	Exeter		homilies	
178.8	Cambridge, Corpus Christi Coll. 422, pp. 1–26	110	70			pp. 1–26	X¹ or X med.			verse and prose dialogue fragments	
179	Cambridge, Corpus Christi Coll. 422, pp. 27–570	111	70			pp. 27–570	XI med.	Winchester NM?	ASMMF 11	computus, titles	
180	Cambridge, Corpus Christi Coll. 449	115	71				XI¹			Ælfric, *Grammar* and *Glossary*	
181	Cambridge, Corpus Christi Coll. 449	115	71				XI			corrections	margins
182	Cambridge, Corpus Christi Coll. 473	116	72			197r	XI²	Winchester OM		note of length	
183	Cambridge, Corpus Christi Coll. 557 + Lawrence, Univ. of Kansas, Kenneth Spencer Research Library, Pryce C2. 1	117	73S				XI med.	Worcester?	ASMMF 7 ASMMF 7	fragments of a homily	
184	Cambridge, Fitzwilliam Museum 45 – 1980	119	7*				X²			55 glosses to Gospels	
185	Cambridge, Fitzwilliam Museum 45 – 1980	119	7*			31v, 46r, 50v, 51v, 52v	X²			7 additional glosses in a smaller hand	
186	Cambridge, Jesus College 15	122	74				XI¹		ASMMF 16	homiletic fragments	
187	Cambridge, Pembroke College 83	134	76			vi r	XI/XII			list of payments	
188	Cambridge, Pembroke College 88	135	77			167v¹⁻⁵	XI¹	Canterbury StA		farming memoranda: list of goods	
189	Cambridge, Pembroke College 88	135	77			i v	XI¹	Canterbury StA		name	*ædwi*
190	Cambridge, Pembroke College 88	135	77			i v	XI¹	Canterbury StA		captions	*min hors*
191	Cambridge, Pembroke College 88	135	77			i v	XI¹	Canterbury StA		scribble	*ælc man*
192	Cambridge, Pembroke College 88	135	77			79r	XI¹	Canterbury StA		scribble	*to huntoþe*

HAND NO.	LIBRARY AND SHELF-MARK	GNEUSS	KER	SAWYER/PELTERET	KER HAND NO.	FOLIOS	DATE	LOCATION	FACSIMILE REFERENCES	CONTENTS	NOTES
193	Cambridge, Pembroke College 88	135	77			168r	XI	Canterbury StA or Bury St Edmunds		name	*RODBEART*
194	Cambridge, Pembroke College 302	139	78	1561		8r	XI²	Hereford		boundaries	
195	Cambridge, Pembroke College 312, C nos 1, 2 + Haarlem, Stadsbiblio-theek 188 F 53 + Sonderhausen, Schlossmuseum Lat. liturg. XI	141	79 79 S G5				XI med.		ASMMF 13 *ASE* 27	continuous psalter gloss	binding strips
196 −199	*unused numbers*										
◆	Cambridge, Queen's College, (Horne) 74, *see now London, BL, Add. 61735*										
200	Cambridge, Queen's College, (Horne) 75 + Oxford, Bodleian Library, Eng. th. c. 74 + Blooming-ton, Indiana Univ., Lilly Library, Poole 40 + New Haven, Yale Univ., Beinecke Library, Osborn fa 26	146	81 81 S				XI in.			homilies and lives of saints	binding strips
201	Cambridge, Sidney Sussex College, Δ. 5. 15	155	82				XI med.	Durham		liturgical directions	
201.5	Cambridge, Trinity College B. 10. 5	173	83			4r	IX?		ASMMF 12	1 gloss to Pauline Epistles	
201.6	Cambridge, Trinity College B. 10. 5	173	83			31r	IX?			1 gloss to Pauline Epistles	
201.7	Cambridge, Trinity College B. 10. 5	173	83			33v	IX			gloss (? English)	
201.8	Cambridge, Trinity College B. 10. 5	173	83			62v, 66v	X			direction to reader	lower margins: *red*
201.9	Cambridge, Trinity College B. 11. 2	174	84			47v¹⁰	X med.	Canterbury StA?	ASMMF 22	2 glosses to Amaralius, *Liber officialis*	
	Cambridge, Trinity College B. 11. 2	174	84			62r²³ right margin	X med.	Canterbury StA?		2 glosses to Amaralius, *Liber officialis*	
202	Cambridge, Trinity College B. 11. 2	174	84	P 92		121v	XI²	Exeter		Leofric ascription	
203	Cambridge, Trinity College B. 14. 3	175	85				XI?	Canterbury CC	ASMMF 12	1 gloss to Arator, *De actibus apostolorum*	

HAND NO.	LIBRARY AND SHELF-MARK	GNEUSS	KER	SAWYER/PELTERET	KER HAND NO.	FOLIOS	DATE	LOCATION	FACSIMILE REFERENCES	CONTENTS	NOTES
204	Cambridge, Trinity College B. 15. 34	177	86				XI med.	Canterbury?	ASMMF 16	homilies	
205	Cambridge, Trinity College B. 15. 34	177	86				XI med.	Canterbury?		contemporary alterations and corrections	
206	Cambridge, Trinity College B. 15. 34	177	86			p. 135	XI med.	Canterbury?		marginal addition	
207	Cambridge, Trinity College B. 15. 34	177	86				XI²			spelling corrections, esp. of *i* to *y*	
208	Cambridge, Trinity College B. 15. 34	177	86			pp. 119–20, 125, 133, 261, 265, 267–76	XI/XII?			later corrections (in two groups)	
209	Cambridge, Trinity College O. 1. 18	188	92			13*r*–17*v*	XI in.		ASMMF 12	9 glosses to Augustine, *Enchiridion*	
210	Cambridge, Trinity College O. 1. 18	188	92			12*r*, 15*r*, 17*r*	XI in.			6 more glosses	
211	Cambridge, Trinity College O. 1. 18	188	92			13*r*–17*r*, 40*r*, 46*v*, 86*r*, 96*v*, 105*r*	XI in.			19 more glosses	
212	Cambridge, Trinity College O. 2. 30, fols. 129–72	189	94			130*v*, 145*r*	XI¹	Canterbury StA	ASMMF 12	2 glosses to the Benedictine Rule	
213	Cambridge, Trinity College O. 2. 30, fols. 129–72	189	94			130*v*, 131*r*, 133*v*, 157*v*	XI¹	Canterbury StA		10 more glosses	
214	Cambridge, Trinity College O. 2. 31	190	95				XI med.	Canterbury CC	ASMMF 12	many glosses to Prosper, *Epigrammata* and to *Disticha Catonis*	
215	Cambridge, Trinity College O. 2. 31	190	95				XI med.	Canterbury CC		a few additional gloses	
216	Cambridge, Trinity College O. 3. 7	193	95*			14*r*, 28*r*	XI¹	Canterbury StA?	ASMMF 12	2 glosses to Boethius, *De consolatione philosophiae*	
217	Cambridge, Trinity College R. 5. 22, fols. 72–158	180	87	1		72*r*–94*r*	X/XI	Sherborne	ASMMF 12	Gregory (Alfred), *Regula pastoralis*	
218	Cambridge, Trinity College R. 5. 22, fols. 72–158	180	87			94*v*–110*v*¹⁵	X/XI	Sherborne		Gregory (Alfred), *Regula pastoralis*	
219	Cambridge, Trinity College R. 5. 22, fols. 72–158	180	87	2		110*v*¹⁵–115*v*	X/XI	Sherborne		Gregory (Alfred), *Regula pastoralis*	

HAND NO.	LIBRARY AND SHELF-MARK	GNEUSS	KER	SAWYER/PELTERET	KER HAND NO.	FOLIOS	DATE	LOCATION	FACSIMILE REFERENCES	CONTENTS	NOTES
220	Cambridge, Trinity College R. 5. 22, fols. 72–158	180	87		3	116r–158	X/XI	Sherborne		Gregory (Alfred), *Regula pastoralis*	
221	Cambridge, Trinity College R. 9. 17, fols. 1–48	182	89				XI/XII			Ælfric, *Grammar, Disticha Catonis*	
222	Cambridge, Trinity College R. 15. 32, pp. 13–36	186	90			pp. 15–26	XI¹	Winchester NM	ASMMF 12	names of months	scribe: *ælsinus* (*ælfsige*)
	London, BL, Cotton Titus D. xxvii	380	202			30r–55r				Ælfric, *De temporibus anni*, computistical notes	
	London, BL, Stowe 944	500	274						EEMF 26	names	main hand
223	Cambridge, Trinity College R. 15. 32, pp. 13–36	186	90			p. 36	XI ex.	Winchester NM		copying note	
224	Cambridge, University Library Add. 3206	30	11				XI²			confessional texts, *Institutes of Polity*, 'Canons of Edgar'	fragment
225	Cambridge, University Library Add. 3330 + London, BL, Add. 50483 K and 71687 + New Haven, Yale Univ., Beinecke Lib. 401 and 401A + Oslo and London, The Schøyen Collection 197 + Philadelphia Free Library, John Frederick Lewis Collection ET 121	857	12S				X²			many glosses to Aldhelm, *De virginitate*, in a small hand	
226	Cambridge, University Library Add. 3330 + London, BL, Add. 50483 K and 71687 + New Haven, Yale Univ., Beinecke Lib. 401 and 401A + Oslo and London, The Schøyen Collection 197 + Philadelphia Free Library, John Frederick Lewis Collection ET 121	857	12S				X²			further glosses in a larger hand	
226.5	Cambridge, University Library, Ely D. C. 1A/1B			794			XI or XI²			bounds and endorsement	late copy or forgery
227	Cambridge, University Library Ff. 1. 23	4	13				XI¹	Canterbury StA? Ramsey?		continuous gloss to psalms and canticles	

HAND NO.	LIBRARY AND SHELF-MARK	GNEUSS	KER	SAWYER/PELTERET	KER HAND NO.	FOLIOS	DATE	LOCATION	FACSIMILE REFERENCES	CONTENTS	NOTES
228	Cambridge, University Library Ff. 1. 23	4	13			5r	XI¹	Canterbury StA? Ramsey?		gloss to psalm 1	
229	Cambridge, University Library Ff. 1. 23	4	13				XI¹	Canterbury StA? Ramsey?		16 additional glosses	
230	Cambridge, University Library Gg. 3. 28	11	15		1		X/XI		ASMMF 17	homilies	main hand
231	Cambridge, University Library Gg. 3. 28	11	15		2	15v^9–16r^{12}, 29v^6–30v^5, 224v^{6-7}, 225r^{29}–225v^1, 225v^{12-14}, 240v^{1-26}, 241r^1–241v^{30}	X/XI			continuations of homilies, Ælfric, *De temporibus anni*, *De paenitentia*, prayers	
232	Cambridge, University Library Gg. 3. 28	11	15			193v–194r	X/XI			words blotted in the text rewritten in margin	
233	Cambridge, University Library Gg. 3. 28	11	15			196r–199v	XI			corrector 1	
234	Cambridge, University Library Gg. 3. 28	11	15			248v–251r	XI			corrector 2	
235	Cambridge, University Library Gg. 3. 28	11	15			59$r^{5, 9, 15}$	XI			corrector 3	
236	Cambridge, University Library Gg. 3. 28	11	15			184v	XI¹			marginal addition	
237	Cambridge, University Library Gg. 5. 35	12	16				XI med.	Canterbury StA?	ASMMF 9	glosses to a verse florilegium by at least two scribes	
238	Cambridge, University Library Hh. 1. 10	13	17		(1)	1v^4–10v^{27}, 13r^1–17v^{27}, 18v^1–20v^{27}, 22r^1–64v^{26}	XI²	Exeter	ASMMF 16	Ælfric's *Grammar* and *Glossary*	
239	Cambridge, University Library Hh. 1. 10	13	17			11r^1–12v^{27}	XI²	Exeter		continuations to *Grammar* and *Glossary*	
240	Cambridge, University Library Hh. 1. 10	13	17		(2)	18r^{1-27}, 21r^1–21v^{27}	XI²	Exeter		continuations to *Grammar* and *Glossary*	

HAND NO.	LIBRARY AND SHELF-MARK	GNEUSS	KER	SAWYER/PELTERET	KER HAND NO.	FOLIOS	DATE	LOCATION	FACSIMILE REFERENCES	CONTENTS	NOTES
241	Cambridge, University Library Hh. I. 10	13	17		3	$65r^1$–$72r^{26}$	XI²	Exeter		continuations to Grammar and Glossary	
242	Cambridge, University Library Hh. I. 10	13	17		4	$72v^1$–$93v^{26}$	XI²	Exeter		continuations to Grammar and Glossary	
243	Cambridge, University Library Hh. I. 10	13	17			e.g. 29v	XI²	Exeter		corrections	
244	Cambridge, University Library Hh. I. 10	13	17			e.g. 26r	XI ex.	Exeter		glosses	
245	Cambridge, University Library Ii. 2. 4	14	19				XI²	Exeter		Gregory (Alfred), *Regula pastoralis*	
246	Cambridge, University Library Ii. 2. 11 + Exeter, Cathedral 3501, fols. 0, 1–7	15	20	P 92		CUL $1r^1$–$1r^2$	XI²	Exeter		Leofric ascription	now recto, formerly verso
247	Cambridge, University Library Ii. 2. 11 + Exeter, Cathedral 3501, fols. 0, 1–7	15	20			CUL $2r^1$–$202r^4$	XI²	Exeter		gospels, Gospel of Nicodemus, *Vindicta salvatoris*	main hand
248	Cambridge, University Library Ii. 2. 11 + Exeter, Cathedral 3501, fols. 0, 1–7	15	20				XI²	Exeter		corrections to gospels	
249	Cambridge, University Library Ii. 2. 11 + Exeter, Cathedral 3501, fols. 0, 1–7	15	20				XI²	Exeter		alterations to gospels	
250	Cambridge, University Library Ii. 2. 11 + Exeter, Cathedral 3501, fols. 0, 1–7	15	20	P 91		Exet. $1r^1$–$2v^2$	XI²	Exeter		record of gifts	
251	Cambridge, University Library Ii. 2. 11 + Exeter, Cathedral 3501, fols. 0, 1–7	15	20	P 91		Exet. $1r^9$, 10, $1v^7$	XI²	Exeter		interlinear additions	
252	Cambridge, University Library Ii. 2. 11 + Exeter, Cathedral 3501, fols. 0, 1–7	15	20	P 99		Exet. 4v	XI/XII	Exeter		manumission	

HAND NO.	LIBRARY AND SHELF-MARK	GNEUSS	KER	SAWYER/PELTERET	KER HAND NO.	FOLIOS	DATE	LOCATION	FACSIMILE REFERENCES	CONTENTS	NOTES
253	Cambridge, University Library Ii. 2. 11 + Exeter, Cathedral 3501, fols. 0, 1–7	15	20	P 101		Exet. $5r^{11-21}$	XI/XII	Exeter		note about bell-ringing	
254	Cambridge, University Library Ii. 2. 11 + Exeter, Cathedral 3501, fols. 0, 1–7	15	20	P 104		Exet. $6r^{1-6}$	XI/XII	Exeter		manumission	
255	Cambridge, University Library Ii. 2. 11 + Exeter, Cathedral 3501, fols. 0, 1–7	15	20	P 105, P 106, P 107		Exet. $6r^{7-25}$	XI/XII	Exeter		3 manumissions	
256	*unused number*										
257	Cambridge, University Library Ii. 2. 11 + Exeter, Cathedral 3501, fols. 0, 1–7	15	20	P 108		Exet. $6r^{26-30}$	XI/XII	Exeter		manumission	
258	Cambridge, University Library Ii. 2. 11 + Exeter, Cathedral 3501, fols. 0, 1–7	15	20	P 109		Exet. $6r^{31-3}$	XI/XII	Exeter		manumission	
259	Cambridge, University Library Ii. 2. 11 + Exeter, Cathedral 3501, fols. 0, 1–7	15	20	P 110		Exet. $6r^{34-6}$	XI/XII	Exeter		manumission	
260	Cambridge, University Library Ii. 2. 11 + Exeter, Cathedral 3501, fols. 0, 1–7	15	20	P 111		Exet. $6r^{37-41}$	XI/XII	Exeter		manumission	
261	Cambridge, University Library Ii. 2. 11 + Exeter, Cathedral 3501, fols. 0, 1–7	15	20	P 112		Exet. $6v^{1-6}$	XI/XII	Exeter		manumission	
262	Cambridge, University Library Ii. 2. 11 + Exeter, Cathedral 3501, fols. 0, 1–7	15	20	P 113		Exet. $6v^{7-15}$	XI/XII	Exeter		manumission	
263	Cambridge, University Library Ii. 2. 11 + Exeter, Cathedral 3501, fols. 0, 1–7	15	20	P 114		Exet. $6v^{16-20}$	XI/XII	Exeter		manumission	

HAND NO.	LIBRARY AND SHELF-MARK	GNEUSS	KER	SAWYER/PELTERET	KER HAND NO.	FOLIOS	DATE	LOCATION	FACSIMILE REFERENCES	CONTENTS	NOTES
264	Cambridge, University Library Ii. 2. 11 + Exeter, Cathedral 3501, fols. 0, 1–7	15	20	P 120–2 and 124–34		Exet. $7r^1$–$7v^{24}$	XI ex. or XI/XII			guild records	
265	Cambridge, University Library Ii. 4. 6	18	21		1	22r–148r	XI med.	Winchester NM		homilies	
266	Cambridge, University Library Ii. 4. 6	18	21		2	7rv, 9r–21v^{10}, 148r–303v, 306rv, 308rv	XI med.	Winchester NM		homilies	
267	Cambridge, University Library Ii. 4. 6	18	21			23v–37r	XI med.	Winchester NM		glosses and additions	
	London, BL, Stowe 2	499	271						ASMMF 2	psalter gloss	main hand
268	Cambridge, University Library Ii. 4. 6	18	21			145r, 229v	XI med.	Winchester NM		directions to reader or copyist	margin
269	Cambridge, University Library Kk. 1. 24 + London, BL, Cotton Tiberius B. v, vol. 1, fols. 74 and 76, + Sloane 1044, fol. 2	21	22			Tib. 74v	X^2	Ely		guild record	
270	Cambridge, University Library Kk. 1. 24 + London, BL, Cotton Tiberius B. v, vol. 1, fols. 74 and 76, + Sloane 1044, fol. 2	21	22			Tib. 74v	X^2	Ely		record	
271	Cambridge, University Library Kk. 1. 24 + London, BL, Cotton Tiberius B. v, vol. 1, fols. 74 and 76, + Sloane 1044, fol. 2	21	22			Tib. 76v	X/XI	Ely		farming memoranda: record of freeholders	
◆	Cambridge, University Library Kk. 3. 18, *see Cambridge, Corpus Christi Coll. 391*										
◆	Cambridge, University Library Kk. 3. 18, *see Cambridge, Corpus Christi Coll. 178, Part A, + Cambridge, Corpus Christi Coll. 162, pp. 139–60*										

HAND NO.	LIBRARY AND SHELF-MARK	GNEUSS	KER	SAWYER/PELTERET	KER HAND NO.	FOLIOS	DATE	LOCATION	FACSIMILE REFERENCES	CONTENTS	NOTES
272	Cambridge, University Library Kk. 3. 18	22	23				XI²			contemporary corrections	
273	Cambridge, University Library Kk. 3. 18	22	23		49v		XI²			interlinear addition	
274	Cambridge, University Library Kk. 3. 18	22	23		63v		XI²			marginal addition	
275	Cambridge, University Library Kk. 3. 21	23	24		104r		XI	Abingdon		names	*byrnstan beoffan sunu, ælfnoð ælrices sunu*
276	Cambridge, University Library Kk. 3. 21	23	24		104r		XI med.	Abingdon		names of winds	
276.5	Cambridge, University Library Kk. 5. 16	25	25							glosses to Bede, *Ecclesiastical History*	
276.7	Cambridge, University Library Kk. 5. 16	25	25		128v		VIII¹ (in or after 737)			Cædmon's Hymn	
277	Cambridge, University Library Kk. 5. 32, fols. 49–60	26	26		60v		XI ex.	Canterbury StA ?		Byrhtferth's *Enchiridion* (part)	
277.3	Cambridge, University Library Ll. 1. 10	28	27		2r¹⁻¹³		IX in.		ASMMF 7	conclusion to exhortation to prayer	
277.5	Cambridge, University Library Ll. 1. 10	28	27		43r–44v		IX in.			75 glosses to *Lorica*	
277.6	Cambridge, University Library Ll. 1. 10	28	27		43r–44v		X med.			further glosses	
277.8	Cambridge, University Library Ll. 1. 10	28	27		57r		X med.			2 glosses to a prayer	
278	Canterbury, Cathedral Library Add. 20	206	97S		1r¹–1v¹⁹		XI²	Canterbury CC ?	ASMMF 5	Rule of Chrodegang	
279	Canterbury, Cathedral Library Add. 25	207	96		1r¹–2v³¹		X ex.	Canterbury CC ?	ASMMF 5	Gregory, *Dialogi*	
280	Canterbury, Cathedral Library Add. 32	208	97*				X in.		ASMMF 5	glosses to Gregory, *Dialogi*	binding fragment

HAND NO.	LIBRARY AND SHELF-MARK	GNEUSS	KER	SAWYER/PELTERET	KER HAND NO.	FOLIOS	DATE	LOCATION	FACSIMILE REFERENCES	CONTENTS	NOTES
281	Canterbury, Cathedral Library, Chart. Ant. A. 207			1472			1044 × 1045			record in English	
282	Canterbury, Cathedral Library, Chart. Ant. B. 1			939			995 × 999			charter in English	
283	Canterbury, Cathedral Library, Chart. Ant. B. 2			1501			XI²			will	
284	Canterbury, Cathedral Library, Chart. Ant. C. 3			1089			XI/XII			writ	
285	Canterbury, Cathedral Library, Chart. Ant. C. 4			P 22	1r¹		1069 × 1071			beginning of writ	
◆	Canterbury, Cathedral Library, Chart. Ant. C. 4, *see Cambridge, Corpus Christi Coll. 173, fols. 1–56*										
285.8	Canterbury, Cathedral Library, Chart. Ant. C. 69			132			XI			endorsement	
286	Canterbury, Cathedral Library, Chart. Ant. C. 70			1530			1042 × 1043			will	
287	Canterbury, Cathedral Library, Chart. Ant. C. 204, no. 2			P 22			XI²			writ	
288	Canterbury, Cathedral Library, Chart. Ant. C. 1279			282			XI			bounds	
288.5	Canterbury, Cathedral Library, Chart. Ant. C. 1280			204			IX med.			charter in English	
289	Canterbury, Cathedral Library, Chart. Ant. C. 1281			1019			1049			bounds	
289.1	Canterbury, Cathedral Library, Chart. Ant. C. 1281			1019	1v		XI med.			endorsement	
289.5	Canterbury, Cathedral Library, Chart. Ant. C. 1282			1445			X¹			'Fonthill letter'	

HAND NO.	LIBRARY AND SHELF-MARK	GNEUSS	KER	SAWYER/PELTERET	KER HAND NO.	FOLIOS	DATE	LOCATION	FACSIMILE REFERENCES	CONTENTS	NOTES
290	Canterbury, Cathedral Library, Chart. Ant. C. 1311			971			XI²	Exeter		bounds	fragment
291	Canterbury, Cathedral Library, Chart. Ant. E. 206			433			XI med. or XI²			bounds	
291.5	Canterbury, Cathedral Library, Chart. Ant. F. 150			350			IX/X			English phrases in Latin charter and English bounds	
292	Canterbury, Cathedral Library, Chart. Ant. H. 68			1503			XI¹			will	
292.8	Canterbury, Cathedral Library, Chart. Ant. H. 130			1276			IX²			bounds	
293	Canterbury, Cathedral Library, Chart. Ant. H. 130			1276			X²			endorsement in the name of King Edgar	
293.5	Canterbury, Cathedral Library, Chart. Ant. M. 14			332			IX med.	Canterbury CC		note in English	
	London, BL, Cotton Augustus ii 16			1196						charter in Latin and English	
	London, BL, Cotton Augustus ii 52			1195						charter in English	
	London, BL, Cotton Augustus ii 66			328						occasional phrases	
	London, BL, Cotton Augustus ii 71			316						bounds	
	London, BL, Cotton Augustus ii 92			1197						endorsement	
	London, BL, Stowe Charter 19			344			IX² (873)			English summary of Latin charter	
294	Canterbury, Cathedral Library, Chart. Ant. R. 14			546			X²?			bounds	
295	Canterbury, Cathedral Library, Chart. Ant. S. 260			959			XI²			charter in English	
296	Canterbury, Cathedral Library, Chart. Ant. T. 37			433			XI² (c. 1069)			bounds	
	Exeter, Cathedral 2528			P 17		$1r^{13}$–$1r^{23}$				bounds and endorsement	
	Oxford, Bodleian Library, Eng. hist. a. 2, no. I			255		$1r^{6-23}$ and dorse				bounds and endorsement	
297	Chelmsford, Essex Record Office, D/DP T 209			704			962			bounds	

HAND NO.	LIBRARY AND SHELF-MARK	GNEUSS	KER	SAWYER/PELTERET	KER HAND NO.	FOLIOS	DATE	LOCATION	FACSIMILE REFERENCES	CONTENTS	NOTES
298	Chichester, West Sussex Record Office Cap. 1/17/I			43			X/XI			bounds and endorsement	
298.5	Cologne, Dombibliothek 213	836	98*			122v	VIII			1 gloss to *Collectio canonum* in margin	
299	Copenhagen, Kongelige Bibliotek Acc 1996/12 + Copenhagen, Rigsarkivet, Aftagne Pergamentfragmenter 637–64, 669–71, 674–98 + The Hague, Koninklijke Bibliotheek 133. D. 22 (21)	811.5 816.6 830	G2 424B 118			Cop. KB 1r, 1v²–2r	XI¹			many binding fragments containing Ælfric homilies set	
300	Copenhagen, Kongelige Bibliotek Acc 1996/12 + Copenhagen, Rigsarkivet, Aftagne Pergamentfragmenter 637–64, 669–71, 674–98 + The Hague, Koninklijke Bibliotheek 133. D. 22 (21)	811.5 816.6 830	G2 424B 118			Cop. KB 1v¹, 2v	XI¹			many binding fragments containing Ælfric homilies set	
301	Copenhagen, Kongelige Bibliotek Acc 1996/12 + Copenhagen, Rigsarkivet, Aftagne Pergamentfragmenter 637–64, 669–71, 674–98 + The Hague, Koninklijke Bibliotheek 133. D. 22 (21)	811.5 816.6 830	G2 424B 118			Cop. Rigsarkiv 2r¹–8r, 8v³⁻¹⁰, 8v²⁵–12v	XI¹			many binding fragments containing Ælfric homilies set	
302	Copenhagen, Kongelige Bibliotek Acc 1996/12 + Copenhagen, Rigsarkivet, Aftagne Pergamentfragmenter 637–64, 669–71, 674–98 + The Hague, Koninklijke Bibliotheek 133. D. 22 (21)	811.5 816.6 830	G2 424B 118			Cop. Rigsarkiv 1rv	XI¹			many binding fragments containing Ælfric homilies set	

HAND NO.	LIBRARY AND SHELF-MARK	GNEUSS	KER	SAWYER/PELTERET	KER HAND NO.	FOLIOS	DATE	LOCATION	FACSIMILE REFERENCES	CONTENTS	NOTES
303	Copenhagen, Kongelige Bibliotek Acc 1996/12	811.5	G2			Cop. Rigsarkiv $8v^{1-2}$, $8v^{11-24}$	XI[1]			many binding fragments containing Ælfric homilies set	
	+ Copenhagen, Rigsarkivet, Aftagne Pergamentfragmenter 637–64, 669–71, 674–98	816.6	424B								
	+ The Hague, Koninklijke Bibliotheek 133. D. 22 (21)	830	118								
304	Copenhagen, Kongelige Bibliotek Acc 1996/12	811.5	G2			Hague $1r–4v$	XI[1]			many binding fragments containing Ælfric homilies set	
	+ Copenhagen, Rigsarkivet, Aftagne Pergamentfragmenter 637–64, 669–71, 674–98	816.6	424B								
	+ The Hague, Koninklijke Bibliotheek 133. D. 22 (21)	830	118								
305	Copenhagen, Kongelige Bibliotek Acc 1996/12	811.5	G2			Cop. Rigsarkiv $1v^9$, $1v^{16}$	XI[1]			2 corrections	
	+ Copenhagen, Rigsarkivet, Aftagne Pergamentfragmenter 637–64, 669–71, 674–98	816.6	424B								
	+ The Hague, Koninklijke Bibliotheek 133. D. 22 (21).	830	118								
306	Copenhagen, Kongelige Bibliotek Acc 1996/12	811.5	G2			Cop. Rigsarkiv $6r^{15}$	XI[1]			1 correction	
	+ Copenhagen, Rigsarkivet, Aftagne Pergamentfragmenter 637–64, 669–71, 674–98	816.6	424B								
	+ The Hague, Koninklijke Bibliotheek 133. D. 22 (21)	830	118								

HAND NO.	LIBRARY AND SHELF-MARK	GNEUSS	KER	SAWYER/PELTERET	KER HAND NO.	FOLIOS	DATE	LOCATION	FACSIMILE REFERENCES	CONTENTS	NOTES
307	Copenhagen, Kongelige Bibliotek G. K. S. 1595	814	99			66*v*	XI in.	Worcester or York	EEMF 25, ASMMF 26	notes for a homily	hand of Archbishop Wulfstan
	London, BL, Add. 38651, fols. 57, 58	294	130			57*v*–58*r*					
	London, BL, Cotton Claudius A. iii, 31–86	314	141			36*v*30, 37*r*2, 37*v*5, 21, 24				interlinear alterations to laws	
	London, BL, Cotton Nero A. i, fols. 70–177	341	164			100*v*1–4, 102*r*1–2, 109*v*, 120*r*8–15			EEMF 17	additions	plus marginalia and alterations
	London, BL, Cotton Tiberius A. xiii	366	190			115*r*–116*r*				additions	
	London, BL, Harley 55, fols. 1–4	412	225			3*v*20, 4*v*4, 4*v*19–20, 4*v*22				interlinear additions to laws and statement concerning land	
	Oxford, Bodleian Library, Hatton 20	626	324			1*r*–2*r*				alterations to Gregory (Alfred), *Regula pastoralis*	
	York, Minster Library, Add. 1, fols. 10–161	774	402			158*r*, 159*v*				interlinear additions to a homily	
308	Copenhagen, Kongelige Bibliotek G. K. S. 2034	815	100				XI1		ASMMF 26	143 glosses to Bede's verse *Vita S. Cuthberti*	
309	Copenhagen, Kongelige Bibliotek G. K. S. 2034	815	100			25*v*	XI1			1 gloss to Pseudo-Columbanus, *Praecepta vivendi*	
310	Copenhagen, Kongelige Bibliotek N. K. S. 167b	816	101				X/XI		ASMMF 26	*Waldere* fragment	
♦	Copenhagen, Rigsarkivet, Aftagne Pergamentfragmenter, *see Copenhagen, Kongelige Bibliotek Acc 1996/12*										
311	Dorchester, Records Office D 124			736		1*r*12–13	965			bounds	
312	Dorchester, Records Office D 124			736		1*v*	X/XI			endorsement	
313	Dorchester, Records Office D 124/1			961			1024–5			bounds	
314	Dorchester, Records Office D 124/2			1004			XI med.			bounds	
314.1	Dorchester, Records Office D 124/2			1004		1*v*	XI med.			endorsement	

HAND NO.	LIBRARY AND SHELF-MARK	GNEUSS	KER	SAWYER/PELTERET	KER HAND NO.	FOLIOS	DATE	LOCATION	FACSIMILE REFERENCES	CONTENTS	NOTES
315	Dublin, Trinity College 174	215	103				XI ex.		ASMMF 5	inscription	*of searbyrig ic eom*
315.5	Durham, Cathedral Library A. II.17, fols. 2–107	220	105			80r, 80*v, 106r	X med.	Chester-le-Street	ASMMF 14	scribbles (*boge mesepreost god preost, boge messepreost god preost, boge messepreost god preost aldred god biscop*)	
316	Durham, Cathedral Library A. IV. 19	223	106			1r–53r, 54r–62v, 70r–71v, 77r–84r, 86r–88v	X²	Chester-le-Street	EEMF 16, ASMMF 14	continuous gloss to collectar, and to liturgical and educational material; corrections to earlier OE; colophon	scribe: Aldred
	London, BL, Cotton Nero D. iv	343	165			3r–259r			Kendrick, 1956; ASMMF 3	continuous gloss to gospels; colophon	
316.9	Durham, Cathedral Library A. IV. 19	223	106			pp. 109–14	IX/X		ASMMF 14	collectar, texts from pontifical services	
317	Durham, Cathedral Library A. IV. 19	223	106			47v	XI¹	Chester-le-Street		liturgical formulae	margin
318	Durham, Cathedral Library B. III. 32	244	107			1r–55v	XI¹	Canterbury	ASMMF 14	gloss to hymnal and monastic canticles	main hand
319	Durham, Cathedral Library B. III. 32	244	107			2rv, 5rv, 9v–10r, 33r, 53r–54r	XI¹	Canterbury		continuous gloss to hymns and canticles	
320	Durham, Cathedral Library B. III. 32	244	107			11v, 12r, 13v, 15v, 18r	XI¹	Canterbury		gloss to hymns	
321	Durham, Cathedral Library B. III. 32	244	107			46r–52v, 54v–55v	XI¹	Canterbury		gloss to canticles	
322	Durham, Cathedral Library B. III. 32	244	107			43v–45v	XI med.	Canterbury		proverbs	
323	Durham, Cathedral Library B. III. 32	244	107			56r–127r	XI¹	Canterbury		Ælfric, *Grammar*	
324	Durham, Cathedral Library B. III. 32	244	107			$62v^{27-30}$	XI¹	Canterbury		intervening hand	
325	Durham, Cathedral Library B. IV. 9	246	108			$7r^{16}$	XI	Durham?	ASMMF 14	1 gloss to Prudentius anthology	
326	Durham, Cathedral Library B. IV. 9	246	108			$14r^{20}$, $15v^{8}$, $22r^{1}$, $77v^{23}$	XI	Durham?		5 more glosses	
327	Durham, Cathedral Library B. IV. 24	248	109			74–123	XI²	Durham	ASMMF 14	Benedictine Rule	
328	Durham, Cathedral Library Muniments 2.1			P 64			1099 × 1100?	Durham		episcopal writ	

HAND NO.	LIBRARY AND SHELF-MARK	GNEUSS	KER	SAWYER/PELTERET	KER HAND NO.	FOLIOS	DATE	LOCATION	FACSIMILE REFERENCES	CONTENTS	NOTES
329	Edinburgh, National Library of Scotland 18. 7. 7	253	III			$1v^9–2r^{12}$	XI in.	Thorney	ASMMF 5	81 glosses to Sedulius, *Carmen paschale*	
330	Edinburgh, National Library of Scotland 18. 7. 7	253	III			$3r^2–36r^3$	X ex.	Thorney		71 more glosses	
331	Edinburgh, University Library, Laing Charter 18			313			XI			charter in English	
332	El Escorial, Real Biblioteca E. II. I	823	115			$1r$	XI^2	Horton, Dorset		inscription	name: *ælfgyþ*
332.5	Èpinal, Bibliothèque Municipale 72, fols. 94–107	824	114				c. 700		ASMMF 18 EEMF 22	glossary	
333	Exeter, Cathedral 2517			389			XI^1	Crediton?		bounds and endorsement	
	Exeter, Cathedral 2519			386						bounds	
	London, BL, Add. Charter 19516			387						bounds	
	Stafford, William Salt Library S. MS 7			433						bounds	
333a	Exeter, Cathedral 2525			971		$1r^{16–18}$	1033	Crediton?		bounds	
333b	London, BL, Cotton Augustus ii 69			963		$1r^{12–14}$	1031	Crediton?		bounds	
334	Exeter, Cathedral 2518			388			XI^2	Exeter?		bounds	
334.2	Exeter, Cathedral 2520			669						bounds	
334.2a	Exeter, Cathedral 2520			669						endorsement	
335	Exeter, Cathedral 2521r			755			XI^2	Exeter		bounds	
	Exeter, Cathedral 2521v			770						bounds	
	Exeter, Cathedral 2527v			832						bounds	
	Oxford, Bodleian Library Auct. F. 3. 6	537	296	P 92	iii	$v^{13–16}$				Leofric ascription	
336	Exeter, Cathedral 2522			684		$1r^{14–15}$	X^2	Exeter?		bounds	
336.1	Exeter, Cathedral 2522			684		$1v$	X^2	Exeter?		endorsement	
337	Exeter, Cathedral 2523			830			X^2 or XI^1	Exeter?		bounds	

HAND NO.	LIBRARY AND SHELF-MARK	GNEUSS	KER	SAWYER/PELTERET	KER HAND NO.	FOLIOS	DATE	LOCATION	FACSIMILE REFERENCES	CONTENTS	NOTES
338	Exeter, Cathedral 2524			951			XI^2			charter with English content and bounds	
339	Exeter, Cathedral 2526			1003		Irv	XI med.			bounds and endorsement	
340	Exeter, Cathedral 2527			1027			XI^2			bounds	
◆	Exeter, Cathedral 2528, *see Canterbury, Cathedral Library, Chart. Ant. T. 37*										
340.5	Exeter, Cathedral 2530			1547			XI^1			bounds	
◆	Exeter, Cathedral 3501, fols. 0, I–7, *see Cambridge, University Library Ii. 2. II*										
341	Exeter, Cathedral 3501, fols. 8–130	257	116				X^2		Chambers, 1933	verse	
342	Exeter, Cathedral 3507	258	116*				XI		ASMMF 22	2 glosses to Isidore, *De natura rerum*	
343	Exeter, Cathedral 3530			1547			XI^1			bounds in English only	fragment
344	Exeter, Cathedral 3530			1547			XI^1			endorsement	
345	Geneva, Bibliotheca Bodmeriana, Bodmer 2	828	285S				XI^2		ASMMF 20	homiletic fragment	fragment
346	Gloucester, Cathedral 35	262	117			I–3, $7r^{1-3}$, $7r^{6}$–7v	XI^1			homiletic fragments	
347	Gloucester, Cathedral 35	262	117			4r–6v	XI med.			Mary of Egypt homily	fragment
348	Gloucester, Cathedral 35	262	117			6v	XI^2			Benedictine Rule	fragment
349	Gloucester, Cathedral 35	262	117			7v	XI^2			addition to homily	margin
◆	The Hague, Koninklijke Bibliotheek 133. D. 22 (21), *see Copenhagen, Kongelige Bibliotek Acc 1996/12*										
350	Hereford, Cathedral Library P. i. 2	266	119	1462		134rv	XI med.			memorandum of dispute over land	
350a	Hereford, Cathedral Library P. i. 2	266	119	1469		135r	XI med.			memorandum of land purchase	

HAND NO.	LIBRARY AND SHELF-MARK	GNEUSS	KER	SAWYER/PELTERET	KER HAND NO.	FOLIOS	DATE	LOCATION	FACSIMILE REFERENCES	CONTENTS	NOTES
351	Hereford, Cathedral Library P. i. 2	266	119			135v	XI			probably another memorandum	largely erased, begins *her*
352	Hertford, Hertfordshire Records Office D/ELW Z (1175)			1031		1r^{15}–1r^{19}	1060			bounds	
352.5	King's Lynn, Corporation Manuscripts, Ae. 34			980			XI/XII			Latin and English charter	
◆	Lawrence, Univ. of Kansas, Pryce mss, *see Cambridge, Corpus Christi Coll 557, London, BL, Harley 3376, and Oxford, Bodleian Library, Hatton 115*										
352.7	Leiden, Universiteitsbibliotheek Vossianus lat. F. 96A					1rv	IX		ASMMF 13	1 gloss and 1 word in the text	probably written by an Anglo-Saxon, perhaps on the continent
353	Lichfield, Cathedral 1	269	123			p. 4	XI^1			land record	margin
354	Lincoln, Cathedral 182	274	124			27v	XI	Abingdon?	ASMMF 21	gloss	top margin: *geþafa nu*
355	Lincoln, Cathedral 298, no. 2	276	125			1r^1–2v^{37}	XI^2			hexateuch fragment	
356	London, BL, Add. 9381	279	126			1r^{31-4}	X^2	Bodmin		manumission	bottom margin
356.6	London, BL, Add. 9381	279	126			7v^{25-29}	X med.	Bodmin		manumission	name: *eadryde cynigc*
356.7	London, BL, Add. 9381	279	126			8r^{1-2}	X med.	Bodmin		manumission	
356.8	London, BL, Add. 9381	279	126			8r^{4-7}	X med.	Bodmin		manumission	
357	London, BL, Add. 9381	279	126	P 87		8r^{8-19}	XI^2	Bodmin		manumission	
358	London, BL, Add. 9381	279	126	P 88		8v^{8-22}	XI^2	Bodmin		manumission	
359	London, BL, Add. 9381	279	126	P 89		133v	XI/XII	Bodmin		manumission	margin
360	London, BL, Add. 9381	279	126			141v^{1-7}	X^2	Bodmin		manumission	
360a	London, BL, Add. 9381	279	126			141v^{8-11}	X^2	Bodmin		manumission	
361	London, BL, Add. 9381	279	126			141v^{12-16}	X^2	Bodmin		manumission	

HAND NO.	LIBRARY AND SHELF-MARK	GNEUSS	KER	SAWYER/PELTERET	KER HAND NO.	FOLIOS	DATE	LOCATION	FACSIMILE REFERENCES	CONTENTS	NOTES
361.5	London, BL, Add. 23211	282	127				IX ex.		ASMMF 19	fragments from binding leaves: royal genealogies; martyrology	
◆	London, BL, Add. 34652, fol. 2, *see London, BL, Cotton Otho B. xi*										
362	London, BL, Add. 34652, fol. 3	288	128				XI²			Rule of Chrodegang fragment	
363	London, BL, Add. 37517	291	129				XI in.	Canterbury	ASMMF 2	continuous psalter gloss	
364	London, BL, Add. 37517	291	129			139*r*	X/XI	Canterbury		rubric in litany	
◆	London, BL, Add. 38651, fols. 57, 58, *see Copenhagen, Kongelige Bibliotek G. K. S. 1595*										
365	London, BL, Add. 40000	295	131			29*r*	XI	Thorney?		2 glosses to Matthew Gospel	
366	London, BL, Add. 40000	295	131			4*r*	XI²	Thorney?		inscription	names: *ælfric, wulfwine, eadgife*
366.5	London, BL, Add. 40000	295	131			10*rv*	XI/XII	Thorney		*Liber vitae*	includes OE phrases; names: *eglaf, ulf, þorð clapes sunu*
366.7	London, BL, Add. 40165 A. 2, fols. 6 and 7	298	132				IX ex. or IX/X		ASMMF 19	martyrology fragment	
367	London, BL, Add. 46204 + London, BL, Cotton Nero E. i, vol. 2, fols. 181–4	344.5					XI²			cartulary fragment with English bounds	for charter numbers, see Sawyer, p. 52
◆	London, BL, Add. 47967, *see Cambridge, Corpus Christi Coll. 173, fols. 1–56*										
368	London, BL, Add. 47967	300	133		2	p. 172	XI	Winchester?	EEMF 3	genealogy of Adam	
369	London, BL, Add. 57337	302	416S				XI	Canterbury CC?		4 glosses to pontifical	
370	London, BL, Add. 61735	302.2	80			$1r^{1-18}$	1007–25	Ely		farming memoranda: list of goods	
371	London, BL, Add. 61735	302.2	80			$1v^{1-12}$	1007–25	Ely		farming memoranda: accounts	

HAND NO.	LIBRARY AND SHELF-MARK	GNEUSS	KER	SAWYER/PELTERET	KER HAND NO.	FOLIOS	DATE	LOCATION	FACSIMILE REFERENCES	CONTENTS	NOTES
372	London, BL, Add. 61735	302.2	80			Ir^{18-25}	1007–25	Ely		farming memoranda: further list of goods	
373	London, BL, Add. 61735	302.2	80			Iv^{13-21}	1007–25	Ely		farming memoranda: rents	
◆	London, BL, Add. Charter 19516, *see Exeter, Cathedral 2517*										
374	London, BL, Add. Charter 19788			67			XI			bounds	
374.4	London, BL, Add. Charter 19789			56			VIII			bounds	
374.6	London, BL, Add. Charter 19791			1281			X^1			charter in English	
375	London, BL, Add. Charter 19792			1326		Ir	969			charter in English	
376	London, BL, Add. Charter 19792			1326		Iv	969			endorsement	name: *eadgar cyng*
377	London, BL, Add. Charter 19793			772			X^2 or XI^1			bounds	
378	London, BL, Add. Charter 19794			1347		Ir^{8-9}	984			record of conversion from loanland to bookland	
379	London, BL, Add. Charter 19794			1347		Iv^{1-7}	984			bounds	
380	London, BL, Add. Charter 19795			1385		Ir^{7-10}	1003–16			bounds	
381	London, BL, Add. Charter 19796			1423		Ir^{1-8}	1016–23 or XI^2			charter in English	
382	London, BL, Add. Charter 19797			1399		Ir^{1-7}	1033–8			charter in English	
383	London, BL, Add. Charter 19798			1393		Ir^{8-13}	1038			bounds	
384	London, BL, Add. Charter 19799			1394		Ir^{1-19}	1042			charter in English	
385	London, BL, Add. Charter 19801			1405		Ir^{7-10}	1058			bounds	
385.1	London, BL, Add. Charter 19801			1405		Iv	1058			endorsement	*to norðtune*
386	London, BL, Add. Charter 19802			1156		Ir^{1-5}	1062			writ	
387	London, BL, Arundel 60	304	134			13r–46v, 53r–119r	XI^2	Winchester NM	ASMMF 2	psalter gloss	
388	London, BL, Arundel 60	304	134			149r	1099	Winchester NM		six ages of the world	

HAND NO.	LIBRARY AND SHELF-MARK	GNEUSS	KER	SAWYER/PELTERET	KER HAND NO.	FOLIOS	DATE	LOCATION	FACSIMILE REFERENCES	CONTENTS	NOTES
389	London, BL, Arundel 155	306	135	1	$171r^1$–$182v^7$	XI med.	Canterbury CC	ASMMF 2	gloss to prayers	
390	London, BL, Arundel 155	306	135	2	$182v^8$–$192v^{23}$	XI med.	Canterbury CC		gloss to prayers	
391	London, BL, Arundel 155	306	135		$177r^{16}$	XI med.	Canterbury CC		single gloss	
392	London, BL, Burney 277, fol. 42	307	136		$42rv$	XI^2			laws	fragment
393	London, BL, Campbell Charter VII. I. a			P 42	$1r^{13-14}$	1088			bilingual diploma	
394	London, BL, Campbell Charter xxi, 5			1088	$1r^{1-3}$	1052–66			writ (part)	
◆	London, BL, Campbell Charter xxi, 5, *see Cambridge, Corpus Christi Coll. 173*									
394.2	London, BL, Cotton Augustus ii 3			89			X			endorsement	*norð stur*
394.4	London, BL, Cotton Augustus ii 4			114			IX/X			endorsement	*godmundes leah*
395	London, BL, Cotton Augustus ii 6			786			X^2			bounds	
395.3	London, BL, Cotton Augustus ii 9			190			IX^1			Latin and English charter	
395.4	London, BL, Cotton Augustus ii 9			190			IX^1			endorsement	
395.5	London, BL, Cotton Augustus ii 10			168			IX^1			bounds	
395.5a	London, BL, Cotton Augustus ii 10			168			IX^1			endorsement	
396	London, BL, Cotton Augustus ii 15			1454			990–2			record of land dispute	
◆	London, BL, Cotton Augustus ii 16, *see Canterbury, Cathedral Library, Chart. Ant. M. 14*									
396.2	London, BL, Cotton Augustus ii 16			1196			IX med.			endorsement	
396.4	London, BL, Cotton Augustus ii 17			1204			IX^2			endorsement	
396.5	London, BL, Cotton Augustus ii 17			1204			X			endorsement	
396.6	London, BL, Cotton Augustus ii 19			1200			IX^2			charter in English	

HAND NO.	LIBRARY AND SHELF-MARK	GNEUSS	KER	SAWYER/PELTERET	KER HAND NO.	FOLIOS	DATE	LOCATION	FACSIMILE REFERENCES	CONTENTS	NOTES
396.8	London, BL, Cotton Augustus ii 21			1438			X			endorsement	
397	London, BL, Cotton Augustus ii 22			898			1001	Coventry?		bounds	
397.5	London, BL, Cotton Augustus ii 23			447			X med.			bounds	
	London, BL, Cotton Augustus ii 62			464						bounds	
	London, BL, Stowe Charter 24			512						bounds	
397.6	London, BL, Cotton Augustus ii 23			447			X med.			endorsement	
398	London, BL, Cotton Augustus ii 24			977			1021–3			bounds	
399	London, BL, Cotton Augustus ii 25			P 28			1081?			charter in English	
399.3	London, BL, Cotton Augustus ii 28			287			IX ex.			Latin charter with English note appended	
399.4	London, BL, Cotton Augustus ii 29			1171			X med.			endorsement	
399.5	London, BL, Cotton Augustus ii 30			117			XI			endorsement	
400	London, BL, Cotton Augustus ii 33			587			X^2			bounds	
401	London, BL, Cotton Augustus ii 34			1530			1042–3			will	
402	London, BL, Cotton Augustus ii 35			1473			1044–8			record of land purchase	
402.5	London, BL, Cotton Augustus ii 37			1438			IX^1			endorsement	
403	London, BL, Cotton Augustus ii 39			690			961?			bounds	added to an existing charter
404	London, BL, Cotton Augustus ii 41			594	1*rv*		X med.			bounds	
404.1	London, BL, Cotton Augustus ii 41			594			X med.			endorsement	
404.2	London, BL, Cotton Augustus ii 42			1510			IX med.			will in English	
404.3	London, BL, Cotton Augustus ii 43			618			X med.			bounds	
404.4	London, BL, Cotton Augustus ii 44			552			X med.			bounds	
	London, BL, Cotton Augustus ii 73			510						bounds	
	London, BL, Cotton Augustus ii 83			528						bounds	
	London, BL, Stowe Charter 25			497						bounds	
	London, BL, Stowe Charter 26			535						bounds	
404.5	London, BL, Cotton Augustus ii 45			624			X med.			bounds	

HAND NO.	LIBRARY AND SHELF-MARK	GNEUSS	KER	SAWYER/PELTERET	KER HAND NO.	FOLIOS	DATE	LOCATION	FACSIMILE REFERENCES	CONTENTS	NOTES
404.6	London, BL, Cotton Augustus ii 45			624			X med.			endorsement	
404.7	London, BL, Cotton Augustus ii 46			1862			X med.?			bounds	fragment
405	London, BL, Cotton Augustus ii 49			1084			1065–6			writ	
◆	London, BL, Cotton Augustus ii 52, *see Canterbury, Cathedral Library, Chart. Ant. M. 14*										
406	London, BL, Cotton Augustus ii 57			546			X²?			bounds	
407	London, BL, Cotton Augustus ii 59			1005	I*rv*		1044			bounds and endorsement	
407.1	London, BL, Cotton Augustus ii 60			296			IX med.			endorsement	
◆	London, BL, Cotton Augustus ii 62, *see London, BL, Cotton Augustus ii 23*										
407.2	London, BL, Cotton Augustus ii 62			464			X med.			endorsement	
407.3	London, BL, Cotton Augustus ii 63			495			X med.			bounds	
407.4	London, BL, Cotton Augustus ii 64			1482			IX¹			will in English	
407.5	London, BL, Cotton Augustus ii 64			1482			IX¹			endorsement	
407.6	London, BL, Cotton Augustus ii 65			425			IX med.			bounds	
◆	London, BL, Cotton Augustus ii 66, *see Canterbury, Cathedral Library, Chart. Ant. M. 14*										
407.7	London, BL, Cotton Augustus ii 66			328			IX med.			endorsement	
408	London, BL, Cotton Augustus ii 68			1044			1042–4			bounds	
◆	London, BL, Cotton Augustus ii 69, *see Exeter, Cathedral 2525*										
409	London, BL, Cotton Augustus ii 70			1471			1045			record of land settlement	
◆	London, BL, Cotton Augustus ii 71, *see Canterbury, Cathedral Library, Chart. Ant. M. 14*										

HAND NO.	LIBRARY AND SHELF-MARK	GNEUSS	KER	SAWYER/PELTERET	KER HAND NO.	FOLIOS	DATE	LOCATION	FACSIMILE REFERENCES	CONTENTS	NOTES
409.1	London, BL, Cotton Augustus ii 71			316			IX med.			endorsement	
409.2	London, BL, Cotton Augustus ii 71			316			IX/X			endorsement	
409.3	London, BL, Cotton Augustus ii 72			1268			IX^1			endorsement	
◆	London, BL, Cotton Augustus ii 73, *see London, BL, Cotton Augustus ii 44*										
409.4	London, BL, Cotton Augustus ii 73			510			X med.			endorsement	
409.5	London, BL, Cotton Augustus ii 74			177			XI			endorsement	
409.6	London, BL, Cotton Augustus ii 75			187			IX^1			endorsement	
409.7	London, BL, Cotton Augustus ii 76			214			IX			bounds	
409.8	London, BL, Cotton Augustus ii 77			175			X			bounds	see also Stowe Charter 11
409.9	London, BL, Cotton Augustus ii 78			1436			IX^1			endorsement	
409.10	London, BL, Cotton Augustus ii 78			1436			X			endorsement	
409.11	London, BL, Cotton Augustus ii 79			1188			IX^1			charter in English	
409.12	London, BL, Cotton Augustus ii 79			1188			IX^1			endorsement	
410	London, BL, Cotton Augustus ii 80			1071			XI^2			writ	
◆	London, BL, Cotton Augustus ii 83, *see London, BL, Cotton Augustus ii 44*										
410.7	London, BL, Cotton Augustus ii 83			528			X med.			endorsement	
411	London, BL, Cotton Augustus ii 84			1225			1038–42			charter in English	
412	London, BL, Cotton Augustus ii 85			1489			1035–40			will	
412.2	London, BL, Cotton Augustus ii 86			230			X			occasional words in bounds	
412.4	London, BL, Cotton Augustus ii 87			40			X			endorsement	
412.6	London, BL, Cotton Augustus ii 88			21			VIII^2			endorsement	
412.8	London, BL, Cotton Augustus ii 89			1203			X			endorsement	

HAND NO.	LIBRARY AND SHELF-MARK	GNEUSS	KER	SAWYER/PELTERET	KER HAND NO.	FOLIOS	DATE	LOCATION	FACSIMILE REFERENCES	CONTENTS	NOTES
413	London, BL, Cotton Augustus ii 90			1467			1037–40			record of land settlement	
413.2	London, BL, Cotton Augustus ii 91			23			VIII^1			endorsement	
413.4	London, BL, Cotton Augustus ii 92			1197			IX med.			charter in English	
◆	London, BL, Cotton Augustus ii 92, *see Canterbury, Cathedral Library, Chart. Ant. M. 14*										
413.5	London, BL, Cotton Augustus ii 93			186			IX^1			bounds	
413.6	London, BL, Cotton Augustus ii 94			188			IX^1			endorsement	
413.8	London, BL, Cotton Augustus ii 95			338			IX^2			endorsement	
414	London, BL, Cotton Augustus ii 96			156			X^2			bounds	palimpsest?
414.2	London, BL, Cotton Augustus ii 97			153			VIII^2			endorsement	
414.3	London, BL, Cotton Augustus ii 100			41			XI			endorsement	
414.4	London, BL, Cotton Augustus ii 101			24			IX			endorsement	
414.5	London, BL, Cotton Caligula A. vii, fols. 11–178	308	137			11r–175v	X^2		ASMMF 1	OHG verse	*heliand*
415	London, BL, Cotton Caligula A. vii, fols. 11–178	308	137			17r	XI^1			title	margin
416	London, BL, Cotton Caligula A. vii, fols. 11–178	308	137			176r–178r	XI^1			verse charm	
417	London, BL, Cotton Caligula A. xiv, fols. 93–130	310	138			93r–121v^{12}, 125r–130v	XI med.		ASMMF 19	lives of saints	5-quire fragment
417a	London, BL, Cotton Caligula A. xiv, fols. 93–130	310	138			121v^{13}–124v	XI med.			larger script but very similar hand	
418	London, BL, Cotton Caligula A. xv, fols. 120–53	411	139			120r^1–132r^{23}, 139r–140v	1073 × 1074	Canterbury CC		computistica, prognostics, charms, notes on bloodletting, ages of the world, ages of Virgin, Christ, Adam and Noah, annals 988–1076, colloquy on celebrating mass	

HAND NO.	LIBRARY AND SHELF-MARK	GNEUSS	KER	SAWYER/PELTERET	KER HAND NO.	FOLIOS	DATE	LOCATION	FACSIMILE REFERENCES	CONTENTS	NOTES
419	London, BL, Cotton Caligula A. xv, fols. 120–53	411	139		135r^{13}		XI^2	Canterbury CC		addition	*7 her com willelm*
420	London, BL, Cotton Caligula A. xv, fols. 120–53	411	139		135r^{31-2}		after 1085	Canterbury CC		added annals	
421	London, BL, Cotton Caligula A. xv, fols. 120–53	411	139		135r^{34}		after 1087	Canterbury CC		added annals	
422	London, BL, Cotton Caligula A. xv, fols. 120–53	411	139		136r^1		after 1089	Canterbury CC		added annals	
423	London, BL, Cotton Caligula A. xv, fols. 120–53	411	139		136r^4		after 1093	Canterbury CC		added annals	
424	London, BL, Cotton Caligula A. xv, fols. 120–53	411	139		136r^5		after 1093	Canterbury CC		added annals	
425	London, BL, Cotton Caligula A. xv, fols. 120–53	411	139		136v^{8-9}		1097 or soon after	Canterbury CC		added annals	
426	London, BL, Cotton Caligula A. xv, fols. 120–53	411	139		136v^{12}		probably after 1100	Canterbury CC		added annals	
427	London, BL, Cotton Caligula A. xv, fols. 120–53	411	139		136v^{10-11}		probably after 1100	Canterbury CC		added annals	
428	London, BL, Cotton Caligula A. xv, fols. 120–53	411	139		142rv–143rv		XI^2	Canterbury CC		Ælfric, *De temporibus anni*; extracts from computus	
429	London, BL, Cotton Caligula A. xv, fols. 120–53	411	139		144r–153v		XI/XII	Canterbury CC		Ælfric, *De temporibus anni*	
429.5	London, BL, Cotton Charter vi 4			266			IX^2			bounds	forged charter
429.8	London, BL, Cotton Charter viii 3			96			VIII^2			endorsement	
430	London, BL, Cotton Charter viii 9			1008	Irv		1045			bounds	
	London, BL, Harley Charter 43 C 8			994	Irv		1042			bounds	
431	London, BL, Cotton Charter viii 11			540	Irv		XI?			bounds	

HAND NO.	LIBRARY AND SHELF-MARK	GNEUSS	KER	SAWYER/PELTERET	KER HAND NO.	FOLIOS	DATE	LOCATION	FACSIMILE REFERENCES	CONTENTS	NOTES
◆	London, BL, Cotton Charter viii 12, *see Cambridge, Corpus Christi Coll. 173, fols. 1–56*										
431.5	London, BL, Cotton Charter viii 12			636			X med.			endorsement	cf. endorsements of S 298, 416, 649, 1008
432	London, BL, Cotton Charter viii 14			864	1r$^{10-15}$		987			bounds	
432.4	London, BL, Cotton Charter viii 16			416			X^1			bounds	scribe 'Athelstan A'
432.5	London, BL, Cotton Charter viii 16			416			X^1			endorsement	
432.7	London, BL, Cotton Charter viii 16			1533			X^1			will in English	
432.8	London, BL, Cotton Charter viii 16			1533			XI^1			endorsement	
433	London, BL, Cotton Charter viii 17			443			XI?			bounds	
434	London, BL, Cotton Charter viii 20			1458			994 × 996			land memorandum	
434.5	London, BL, Cotton Charter viii 22			449			X med.			bounds	
434.6	London, BL, Cotton Charter viii 22			449			X med.			endorsement	
435	London, BL, Cotton Charter viii 28			706	1rv		962			bounds	scribe: 'Edgar A'
	London, BL, Harley Charter 43 C 3			703	1rv		962				
	London, BL, Stowe Charter 29			717	1rv		963				
435.8	London, BL, Cotton Charter viii 29			327	1r		IX^2			bounds	
	London, BL, Cotton Charter viii 32			331						bounds	
435.9	London, BL, Cotton Charter viii 29			327	1v		X			endorsement	
436	London, BL, Cotton Charter viii 29			327	1r$^{37-40}$		X/XI?			late endorsement	
436.2	London, BL, Cotton Charter viii 30			280			X			endorsement	
436.4	London, BL, Cotton Charter viii 31			165			X			endorsement	
437	London, BL, Cotton Charter viii 33			671	1r^{16} and interlinear		X/XI	Rochester?		additional bounds	
438	London, BL, Cotton Charter viii 33			671	1r$^{17-19}$, 1v		X ex.	Rochester?		bounds	
438.5	London, BL, Cotton Charter viii 34			35			VIII^2			bounds	

HAND NO.	LIBRARY AND SHELF-MARK	GNEUSS	KER	SAWYER/PELTERET	KER HAND NO.	FOLIOS	DATE	LOCATION	FACSIMILE REFERENCES	CONTENTS	NOTES
438.6	London, BL, Cotton Charter viii 34			35			X			endorsement	
439	London, BL, Cotton Charter viii 35			308			XI ?			bounds and endorsement	
439.5	London, BL, Cotton Charter viii 36			298			IX^1 or IX med.			bounds	
440	London, BL, Cotton Charter viii 37			1460		$1r^{1-16}$	1010 × 1023			land memorandum (record of dispute)	
440.5	London, BL, Cotton Charter viii 38			1539			X/XI			will in English	
441	London, BL, Cotton Charter xi 51			P63			XI ex.			bounds	
442	London, BL, Cotton Charter xvi 31			P62			1071 × 1082			writ (fire-damaged)	
443	London, BL, Cotton Claudius A. i, fols. 5–36	312	140			11r	X/XI or X^2	Glastonbury?		1 gloss to Frithegod's life of Wilfrid	
444	London, BL, Cotton Claudius A. i, fols. 5–36	312	140			13v, 14v, 31r	X^2	Glastonbury?		3 more glosses	
445	London, BL, Cotton Claudius A. iii, fols. 4–6	362	185	914		$4r^{1}$–$6r^{5}$	XI^1	Canterbury CC		refoundation charter	scribe: *Eadui Basan*
	London, BL, Royal I D. IX	447	247			$44v^{1-13}$				writ	
	London, BL, Stowe Charter 38			950		$1r^{15-19}$				bounds	
446	London, BL, Cotton Claudius A. iii, fol. 5v	362	185	1090		5v	XI^2	Canterbury CC		writ in lower margin	
447	London, BL, Cotton Claudius A. iii, fol. 6	362	185	1047, 1222, 1229, 1389		$6r^{8}$–$6v^{7}$	XI med.	Canterbury CC		charters in English	
448	London, BL, Cotton Claudius A. iii, fol. 6	362	185	1047		$6v^{8-19}$	XI med.	Canterbury CC		general confirmation of lands and anathema	middle of charter in English
449	London, BL, Cotton Claudius A. iii, fol. 6	362	185	1047		$6v^{20-31}$	XI med.	Canterbury CC		list of estates	end of charter in English
450	London, BL, Cotton Claudius A. iii, fols. 31–86, 106–50	314	141			31v	X/XI			inscription	name: *þureð*

HAND NO.	LIBRARY AND SHELF-MARK	GNEUSS	KER	SAWYER/PELTERET	KER HAND NO.	FOLIOS	DATE	LOCATION	FACSIMILE REFERENCES	CONTENTS	NOTES
451	London, BL, Cotton Claudius A. iii, fols. 31–86, 106–50	314	141			35v^1–38v^5	XI^1			laws	
◆	London, BL, Cotton Claudius A. iii, fols. 31–86, 106–50, *see Copenhagen, Kongelige Bibliotek G. K. S. 1595*										
452	London, BL, Cotton Claudius B. iv	315	142	1		1r–20v, 56v–155v	XI^1		ASMMF 7, EEMF 18	hexateuch	
453	London, BL, Cotton Claudius B. iv	315	142	2		21r–56r	XI^1			hexateuch	
453.4	London, BL, Cotton Cleopatra A. iii	319	143			5r–75va^9	X med.			glossaries	
453.6	London, BL, Cotton Cleopatra A. iii	319	143			75va^{10}–117ra	X med.			glossaries	
454	London, BL, Cotton Cleopatra B. xiii, fols. 1–58 + London, Lambeth Palace Library 489	322 520	144 283	Cleo. 1		Cleo. 2r^1–12r^{19}	XI^2	Exeter	ASMMF 8 ASMMF 8	homilies	
455	London, BL, Cotton Cleopatra B. xiii, fols. 1–58 + London, Lambeth Palace Library 489	322 520	144 283	Cleo. 2		Cleo. 13r^1–31r^2	XI^2	Exeter		homilies	
455a	London, BL, Cotton Cleopatra B. xiii, fols. 1–58 + London, Lambeth Palace Library 489	322 520	144 283	Cleo. 6		Cleo. 57v^{1-21}	XI^2	Exeter		homilies	
456	London, BL, Cotton Cleopatra B. xiii, fols. 1–58 + London, Lambeth Palace Library 489	322 520	144 283	Cleo. 3		Cleo. 31r^3–38r^3	XI^2	Exeter		homilies	
457	London, BL, Cotton Cleopatra B. xiii, fols. 1–58 + London, Lambeth Palace Library 489	322 520	144 283	Cleo. 5		Cleo. 56r^1–57r^{17}	XI^2	Exeter		coronation oath	
458	London, BL, Cotton Cleopatra B. xiii, fols. 1–58 + London, Lambeth Palace Library 489	322 520	144 283	Cleo. 7		Cleo. 58r^2–58r^{11}	XI^2	Exeter		homilies	
459	London, BL, Cotton Cleopatra B. xiii, fols. 1–58 + London, Lambeth Palace Library 489	322 520	144 283	Cleo. 8, Lamb. 3		Cleo. 58r^{12}–58v^{11}, Lamb. 25r^1–31r^2	XI^2	Exeter		Ælfric's paternoster and creed, homilies	

HAND NO.	LIBRARY AND SHELF-MARK	GNEUSS	KER	SAWYER/PELTERET	KER HAND NO.	FOLIOS	DATE	LOCATION	FACSIMILE REFERENCES	CONTENTS	NOTES
460	London, BL, Cotton Cleopatra B. xiii, fols. 1–58 + London, Lambeth Palace Library 489	322 520	144 283	Lamb. 1		Lamb. 1r¹–20r¹⁹	XI²	Exeter		homilies	
461	London, BL, Cotton Cleopatra B. xiii, fols. 1–58 + London, Lambeth Palace Library 489	322 520	144 283	Lamb. 2		20v¹–24v²⁰	XI²	Exeter		added homily	
462	London, BL, Cotton Cleopatra B. xiii, fols. 1–58 + London, Lambeth Palace Library 489	322 520	144 283	Lamb. 4		31r³–46v²⁵	XI²	Exeter		homilies	
463	London, BL, Cotton Cleopatra B. xiii, fols. 1–58 + London, Lambeth Palace Library 489	322 520	144 283	Lamb. 5		47r¹–58v²	XI²	Exeter		homilies	
◆	London, BL, Cotton Cleopatra B. xiii, fols. 1–58, *see Cambridge, Corpus Christi Coll. 191*										
464	London, BL, Cotton Cleopatra C. viii, fols. 4–37	324	145				XI	Canterbury CC		titles to illustrations	
465	London, BL, Cotton Cleopatra C. viii, fols. 4–37	324	145				XI	Canterbury CC		glosses to Prudentius, *Psychomachia*, in more than 1 hand	
466	London, BL, Cotton Domitian i, fols. 2–55	326	146			2r¹⁻²	X/XI	Canterbury StA		8 glosses to Isidore, *De natura rerum*	
467	London, BL, Cotton Domitian i, fols. 2–55	326	146			31v¹⁰, 31v¹¹, 34v²	X²	Canterbury StA	ASMMF 5	3 more glosses to Isidore	
468	London, BL, Cotton Domitian i, fols. 2–55	326	146			53v¹⁰, 53v²¹	XI¹	Canterbury StA		3 glosses to Bede, *De die iudicii*	
469	London, BL, Cotton Domitian i, fols. 2–55	326	146			55v⁴⁻⁶	X²	Canterbury StA		recipe	
470	London, BL, Cotton Domitian i, fols. 2–55	326	146			55v⁷⁻¹²	X/XI	Canterbury StA		booklist	name: *æþelstanes* (genitive)
471	London, BL, Cotton Domitian vii	327	147			47r¹³⁻²⁴	XI med.	Durham	Surtees Soc. 136	manumission	runs into bottom margin

HAND NO.	LIBRARY AND SHELF-MARK	GNEUSS	KER	SAWYER/PELTERET	KER HAND NO.	FOLIOS	DATE	LOCATION	FACSIMILE REFERENCES	CONTENTS	NOTES
472	London, BL, Cotton Domitian vii	327	147	1660	47$v$$^{1-10}$	X ex.	Durham		land grant	name: *þureð*
473	London, BL, Cotton Domitian vii	327	147	1660	47v^{6}	X/XI	Durham		addition	1 interlinear word
474	London, BL, Cotton Domitian vii	327	147	1659, 1661	47$v$$^{11-15}$	XI in.	Durham		2 land grants	names: *norðman, ulfcytel osulfes sunu*
475	London, BL, Cotton Domitian vii	327	147	1661	47$v$$^{16-18}$	XI^1	Durham		later addition to previous	
◆	London, BL, Cotton Domitian viii, *see Cambridge, Corpus Christi Coll. 173*										
476	London, BL, Cotton Domitian ix, fols. 2–7	329	149		4r, 7r	XI^1 ?	Canterbury CC		2 glosses to Aldhelm, *Epistola ad Ehfridum*	
476.7	London, BL, Cotton Domitian ix, fol. 11	329	151		11$r$$^{1-11}$	IX/X			Bede, *Ecclesiastical History*, extract	
476.7a	London, BL, Cotton Domitian ix, fol. 11	329	151		11$r$$^{13-17, 19-29}$	IX/X			further extracts	
476.8	London, BL, Cotton Domitian ix, fol. 11	329	151		11v	IX/X			5 rune names	
477	London, BL, Cotton Domitian ix, fol. 11	330	151		11v	XI/XII			rune names	
478	London, BL, Cotton Faustina A. x, fols. 3–101	331	154		3r–100v^{21}	XI^2		ASMMF 15	Ælfric, *Grammar* and *Glossary*	manuscript from scriptorium of Bodl. Hatton 115
479	London, BL, Cotton Faustina A. x, fols. 3–101	331	154		3r	XI^2			addition to text	margin
479.5	London, BL, Cotton Faustina A. x, fols. 3–101	331	154		32rv, 33rv, etc.	XI^2			many corrections in second half of grammar	
480	London, BL, Cotton Faustina A. x, fols. 3–101	331	154		92v–100v	XI/XII			added glosses in glossary	
481	London, BL, Cotton Faustina A. x, fols. 3–101	331	154		100$v$$^{21-8}$	XI ex.			proverb and 2 maxims	

HAND NO.	LIBRARY AND SHELF-MARK	GNEUSS	KER	SAWYER/PELTERET	KER HAND NO.	FOLIOS	DATE	LOCATION	FACSIMILE REFERENCES	CONTENTS	NOTES
482	London, BL, Cotton Faustina B. iii, fols. 158–98 + London, BL, Cotton Tiberius A. iii, fols. 174–7	332	155			174r–176v	XI med.	Canterbury CC		*Regularis concordia*, ch. 14–19	
483	London, BL, Cotton Faustina B. iii, fols. 158–98 + London, BL, Cotton Tiberius A. iii, fols. 174–7	332	155			Faust. 198v; Tib. 177v	XI med.	Canterbury CC		3 formula letters of death	
484	London, BL, Cotton Galba A. xiv	333	157		I	104r–107v, 111rv, 112v–114r	XI¹	Winchester?	ASMMF 1	prayers	
485	London, BL, Cotton Galba A. xiv	333	157		2	4v⁵–6r⁷	XI¹	Winchester?		prayer for victory	
486	London, BL, Cotton Galba A. xiv	333	157			6r⁸⁻¹³	XI¹	Winchester?		rubric to prayer	
487	London, BL, Cotton Galba A. xiv	333	157			7rv	XI¹	Winchester?		fragmentary confessional text in margin	
488	London, BL, Cotton Galba A. xiv	333	157			118r¹–118v⁷	XI¹	Winchester?		medical recipes	
489	London, BL, Cotton Galba A. xiv	333	157			72r	XI¹	Winchester?		English interventions in Latin medical recipe	
490	London, BL, Cotton Galba A. xiv	333	157			136r¹⁻⁶, 139rv	XI¹	Winchester?		medical recipes on use of badger parts	
491	London, BL, Cotton Galba A. xiv	333	157			27r, 34r	XI¹	Winchester?		4 glosses to prayers	
492	London, BL, Cotton Julius A. ii, fols. 10–135	336	158				XI med.		ASMMF 15	Ælfric, *Grammar* and *Glossary*	
493	London, BL, Cotton Julius A. vi	337	160				XI med.	Canterbury CC	ASMMF 4	continuous gloss to hymns and canticles	
	London, BL, Cotton Vespasian D. xii	391	208		2	92v–102v			ASMMF 4		copy of Julius
494	London, BL, Cotton Julius A. x, fols. 44–175	338	161		I	44r–129v	X/XI		ASMMF 19	martyrology fragment	
495	London, BL, Cotton Julius A. x, fols. 44–175	338	161		2	130r¹–134r¹⁷, 138v¹–145r⁹, 146r¹–153v⁹,	X/XI			martyrology fragment	

HAND NO.	LIBRARY AND SHELF-MARK	GNEUSS	KER	SAWYER/PELTERET	KER HAND NO.	FOLIOS	DATE	LOCATION	FACSIMILE REFERENCES	CONTENTS	NOTES
496	London, BL, Cotton Julius A. x, fols. 44–175	338	161		3	134v^1–138r^{17}, 145r^9–145v^{17}, 153v^{10}–156r^{11}	X/XI			martyrology fragment	
497	London, BL, Cotton Julius A. x, fols. 44–175	338	161		4	156r^{12}–175v	X/XI			martyrology fragment	
498	London, BL, Cotton Julius E. vii	339	162				XI in.		ASMMF 19	saints' lives	main hand
499	London, BL, Cotton Julius E. vii	339	162			107v^{16}–116v	XI in.			*Seven Sleepers* (part)	
499a	London, BL, Cotton Julius E. vii	339	162			116v–136r^{19}	XI in.			rest of *Seven Sleepers* and *Mary of Egypt*	
500	London, BL, Cotton Julius E. vii	339	162			45v	XI in.			two lines in body of text	
501	London, BL, Cotton Julius E. vii	339	162			11v–13v, 14v, 15r, 16r, 24r, 48r, 54r, 60r–65r, 66r, 67rv, 69v–72r, 77r–79r, 80v–82r, 85v, 86v–88r, 89r–90v, 93v–98v, 99v–102v, 104rv, 106r–122v, 139v–143v, 144r–145v, 146v–150v, 153rv, 154v–155v, 156v–157v, 170r, 203v–205v, 206v, 207r	XI^1			main corrector	
502	London, BL, Cotton Julius E. vii	339	162			71r^3, 87r^{20}, 173v^6, 174r^{24}	XI			later corrector	
502a	London, BL, Cotton Julius E. vii	339	162			103v^{22}	XI			another?	
503	London, BL, Cotton Julius E. vii	339	162			173r^{13}, 174r^{13}	XI			different corrector	
504	London, BL, Cotton Nero A. i, fols. 3–57	340	163			3r–41r	XI^2		EEMF 17	laws	
505	London, BL, Cotton Nero A. i, fols. 3–57	340	163			42r–57v	XI^2			laws	

HAND NO.	LIBRARY AND SHELF-MARK	GNEUSS	KER	SAWYER/PELTERET	KER HAND NO.	FOLIOS	DATE	LOCATION	FACSIMILE REFERENCES	CONTENTS	NOTES
506	London, BL, Cotton Nero A. i, fols. 70–177	341	164		1	70r–96v	XI in.	York (or Worcester)	EEMF 17	institutes of polity, homilies, laws	
507	London, BL, Cotton Nero A. i, fols. 70–177	341	164		2	97r–100r, 122r–167v	XI in.	York (or Worcester)		polity	
508	London, BL, Cotton Nero A. i, fols. 70–177	341	164		3	100v–105v	XI in.	York (or Worcester)		polity	
509	London, BL, Cotton Nero A. i, fols. 70–177	341	164		4	109r–120r	XI in.	York (or Worcester)		polity, homilies, laws	
510	London, BL, Cotton Nero A. i, fols. 70–177	341	164			71r$^{1-3}$	XI	York (or Worcester)		addition in a compressed hand	
511	London, BL, Cotton Nero A. i, fols. 70–177	341	164			72v$^{14-15}$	XI	York?		alteration	
512	London, BL, Cotton Nero A. i, fols. 70–177	341	164				XI	York (or Worcester)		corrections perhaps by more than one hand	margins and interlinear
◆	London, BL, Cotton Nero A. i, fols. 70–177, *see Copenhagen, Kongelige Bibliotek G. K. S. 1595*										
◆	London, BL, Cotton Nero D. iv, *see Durham, Cathedral Library A. IV. 19*										
◆	London, BL, Cotton Nero E. i, Pt 1, Pt 2, 1–180, 187–8, *see Cambridge, Corpus Christi Coll. 9*										
◆	London, BL, Cotton Nero E. i, vol. 2, fols. 181–4, *see London, BL, Add. 46204*										
513	*unused number*										
514	London, BL, Cotton Nero E. i, vol. 2, fols. 185–6	345	166			185v–186v	X/XI	Worcester?		laws	fragment

HAND NO.	LIBRARY AND SHELF-MARK	GNEUSS	KER	SAWYER/PELTERET	KER HAND NO.	FOLIOS	DATE	LOCATION	FACSIMILE REFERENCES	CONTENTS	NOTES
514.5	London, BL, Cotton Otho A. vi, fols. 1–129	347	167				X med.			OE Boethius	damaged in the Cotton fire
515	London, BL, Cotton Otho A. viii, fols. 7–34 + London, BL, Cotton Otho B. x, fol. 66	348	168				XI in.	Canterbury StA		Life of St Machutus	
516	London, BL, Cotton Otho A. xviii, fol. 131	352	174				XI¹			homily	fragment
517	London, BL, Cotton Otho B. ii + London, BL, Cotton Otho B. x, fols. 61, 63–4	353	175			1*r*–18*r*¹⁰	X/XI	London?		Gregory (Alfred), *Regula pastoralis*	
518	London, BL, Cotton Otho B. ii + London, BL, Cotton Otho B. x, fols. 61, 63–4	353	175			18*r*¹⁰–18*v*, 43*r*–46*v*	X/XI	London?		Gregory (Alfred), *Regula pastoralis*	
519	London, BL, Cotton Otho B. ii + London, BL, Cotton Otho B. x, fols. 61, 63–4	353	175			19*r*–25*r*	X/XI	London?		Gregory (Alfred), *Regula pastoralis*	
520	London, BL, Cotton Otho B. ii + London, BL, Cotton Otho B. x, fols. 61, 63–4	353	175			25*v*–42*v*	X/XI	London?		Gregory (Alfred), *Regula pastoralis*	
521	London, BL, Cotton Otho B. ii + London, BL, Cotton Otho B. x, fols. 61, 63–4	353	175			47*r*–52*v*, B. x 61, 63–4	X/XI	London?		Gregory (Alfred), *Regula pastoralis*	
522	London, BL, Cotton Otho B. x, except fols. 29–30, 51, 55, 58, 61–4, 66, + Oxford, Bodleian Library, Rawlinson Q. e. 20	355	177		1	'60'–'7' (incl. Rawl.), '10'–'25' (Wanley's enumeration)	XI¹			homilies and lives of saints	fragments
523	London, BL, Cotton Otho B. x, except fols. 29–30, 51, 55, 58, 61–4, 66, + Oxford, Bodleian Library, Rawlinson Q. e. 20	355	177		2	'67'–'9', '57'–'34+35'	XI¹			homilies and lives of saints	fragments
524	London, BL, Cotton Otho B. x, except fols. 29–30, 51, 55, 58, 61–4, 66, + Oxford, Bodleian Library, Rawlinson Q. e. 20	355	177		3	'37'–'44'	XI¹			homilies and lives of saints	fragments

HAND NO.	LIBRARY AND SHELF-MARK	GNEUSS	KER	SAWYER/PELTERET	KER HAND NO.	FOLIOS	DATE	LOCATION	FACSIMILE REFERENCES	CONTENTS	NOTES
525	London, BL, Cotton Otho B. x, except fols. 29–30, 51, 55, 58, 61–4, 66, + Oxford, Bodleian Library, Rawlinson Q. e. 20	355	177		4	'45'	XI[1]			homilies and lives of saints	fragments
526	London, BL, Cotton Otho B. x, fols. 29–30	356	178				XI med.	Worcester?		homily	fragment
◆	London, BL, Cotton Otho B. xi + Cotton Otho B. x, fols. 55, 58, 62, *see Cambridge, Corpus Christi Coll. 173, fols. 1–56*										
527	London, BL, Cotton Otho B. xi + London, BL, Cotton Otho B. x, fols. 55, 58, 62 + London, BL, Add. 34652, fol. 2	357	180		2	B. xi. 35–6, 39–47, 49–50, 52–3, Add. 2*rv*	XI[1]	Winchester		fragments of OE Bede, *ASC* G, WS genealogy	
528	London, BL, Cotton Otho B. xi, fols. 48, 51	357	180		3	B. xi. 48, 51	XI[1]	Winchester		laws	
529	London, BL, Cotton Otho B. xi?	357	180			tiny unnumbered fragment				6 OE words, leaf marked as from Otho B xi	*þu eac swilce / þam welan ea*
530	London, BL, Cotton Otho C. i, vol. 1 + Otho B. x, fol. 51	358	181			1*r*–68*r*[4], 70*r*–110*r*; B.x. 51*rv*	XI[1]	Malmesbury?	ASMMF 3	gospels	main hand; scribe: *wulfwi*
531	London, BL, Cotton Otho C. i, vol. 1	358	181			68*r*[5]–69*r*[4]	XI med.	Malmesbury?		papal bull (part)	
532	London, BL, Cotton Otho C. i, vol. 1	358	181			69*r*[5]–69*v*	XI med.	Malmesbury?		papal bull (conclusion)	
533	London, BL, Cotton Otho C. i, vol. 2	359	182			1*r*–61*v*	XI[1]		ASMMF 6	Gregory's *Dialogi*, bks 1 and 2	
534	London, BL, Cotton Otho C. i, vol. 2	359	182			62*r*–139*v*[4]	XI med.	Worcester		*Dialogi*, bks 3 and 4 (incomplete), *Vitas patrum*	
535	London, BL, Cotton Otho C. i, vol. 2	359	182			139*v*[5]–148*v*	XI med.	Worcester		*Vitas patrum*, letter, homily	
536	London, BL, Cotton Otho C. i, vol. 2	359	182			149*r*–155*v*	XI med.	Worcester		homilies	
537	London, BL, Cotton Otho C. i, vol. 2	359	182			1*r*	XI[2]	Worcester		alteration	name (? *wulfsige*) alt. to *wulfstan*
538	London, BL, Cotton Otho C. i, vol. 2	359	182			113*rv*, 132*v*, 115*r*, 116*r*, 131*r*	XI[2]	Worcester		running titles	

HAND NO.	LIBRARY AND SHELF-MARK	GNEUSS	KER	SAWYER/PELTERET	KER HAND NO.	FOLIOS	DATE	LOCATION	FACSIMILE REFERENCES	CONTENTS	NOTES
539	London, BL, Cotton Otho E. i	360	184				X/XI	Canterbury StA		Lat.–OE glossary	fragments
540	London, BL, Cotton Tiberius A. iii, fols. 2–173	363	186		3	2r–27v, 37v–42v, 60v–64v, 65v–95v	XI med.	Canterbury CC		continuous glosses to *Regularis concordia* and Ælfric, *Colloquy*, prognostics, Ælfric, *De temporibus anni*, notes on the size of Noah's ark, St Peter's, Solomon's temple, homiletic and confessional texts	
541	London, BL, Cotton Tiberius A. iii, fols. 2–173	363	186		4	27v–37v, 46v–56v, 96r–107v, 118r–168v	XI med.	Canterbury CC		continuous gloss to Benedictine Rule and prognostics, prayers, confessional and homiletic texts, lapidiary, Alcuin's *De virtutibus et vitiis*, charm	
542	London, BL, Cotton Tiberius A. iii, fols. 2–173	363	186		5	43r–45r	XI med.	Canterbury CC		notes on Adam, Noah, Ages of the World, Friday fasts, Age of the Virgin, prayers	
542.5	London, BL, Cotton Tiberius A. iii, fols. 2–173	363	186		1	58r–59v	XI med.	Canterbury CC		directions to prayers and charm	
543	London, BL, Cotton Tiberius A. iii, fols. 2–173	363	186			27v12–13, 55v, 56r, 73v–77v, 88v–93v, 118r, 124v3–9	XI2	Canterbury CC		additions to glosses and alterations in a tiny script	
544	London, BL, Cotton Tiberius A. iii, fols. 2–173	363	186			73r–77v	XI2	Canterbury CC		additional alterations in a larger and darker script	
545	London, BL, Cotton Tiberius A. iii, fols. 2–173	363	186			164r	XI ex.	Canterbury CC		name (of owner?)	*eadwi*
546	London, BL, Cotton Tiberius A. iii, fol. 179	363.2	187			179rv	X ex.			horologium	
546.5	London, BL, Cotton Tiberius A. vi, fols. 1–35 + London, BL, Cotton Tiberius A. iii, fol. 178	364	188			Tib. A. vi. 1r–34r; A. iii. 178r	X2 (after 977)	Abingdon?		chronicle, genealogy	*ASC* B
547	London, BL, Cotton Tiberius A. vii, fols. 165–6	365	189				XI1			glosses to Prosper, *Epigrammata*, *Versus ad coniugem*	fragment
548	London, BL, Cotton Tiberius A. xiii	366	190			47r–62v, 98r, 101rv, 111r–113r	XI1	Worcester		cartulary	

HAND NO.	LIBRARY AND SHELF-MARK	GNEUSS	KER	SAWYER/PELTERET	KER HAND NO.	FOLIOS	DATE	LOCATION	FACSIMILE REFERENCES	CONTENTS	NOTES
548a	London, BL, Cotton Tiberius A. xiii	366	190			1*r*–8*v*	XI¹	Worcester		cartulary	
549	London, BL, Cotton Tiberius A. xiii	366	190			9*r*–20*r*, 22*v*–32*v*	XI¹	Worcester		cartulary	
550	London, BL, Cotton Tiberius A. xiii	366	190			39*r*–44*r*	XI¹	Worcester		cartulary	
551	London, BL, Cotton Tiberius A. xiii	366	190			63*r*–101*v*	XI¹	Worcester		cartulary	
552	London, BL, Cotton Tiberius A. xiii	366	190			103*r*–109*v*	XI¹	Worcester		cartulary	
553	London, BL, Cotton Tiberius A. xiii	366	190			109*v*	XI¹	Worcester		note of dues	
554	London, BL, Cotton Tiberius A. xiii	366	190				XI¹	Worcester		headings to charters in cartulary	
555	London, BL, Cotton Tiberius A. xiii	366	190			115*r*–116*v*	XI¹	Worcester		homily	
◆	London, BL, Cotton Tiberius A. xiii, *see Copenhagen, Kongelige Bibliotek G. K. S. 1595*										
◆	London, BL, Cotton Tiberius A. xiii, *see Cambridge, Corpus Christi Coll. 391*										
556	London, BL, Cotton Tiberius A. xiii	366	190			178*r*–189*v*, 180*v*–181*v*	XI²	Worcester		cartulary and note on Bishop *Wlstan* of Worcester	
557	London, BL, Cotton Tiberius A. xiii	366	190			126–77, 191–200	XI²	Worcester		cartulary	
558	London, BL, Cotton Tiberius A. xiii	366	190			190*r*	XI²	Worcester		anathema	
559	London, BL, Cotton Tiberius B. i	370 / 370.2	191		1	3*r*–32*r*²⁵	XI¹	Abingdon?	ASMMF 10	Orosius	
560	London, BL, Cotton Tiberius B. i	370 / 370.2	191		2	32*v*¹–34*v*¹³	XI¹	Abingdon?		Orosius	
561	London, BL, Cotton Tiberius B. i	370 / 370.2	191		3	34*v*¹³–45*r*³	XI¹	Abingdon?		Orosius	
562	London, BL, Cotton Tiberius B. i	370 / 370.2	191		4	45*r*⁴–111*v*	XI¹	Abingdon?		Orosius	
563	London, BL, Cotton Tiberius B. i	370 / 370.2	191			112*r*–118*v*	XI med.	Abingdon?		metrical calendar, gnomic verses, *ASC* C (start)	

HAND NO.	LIBRARY AND SHELF-MARK	GNEUSS	KER	SAWYER/PELTERET	KER HAND NO.	FOLIOS	DATE	LOCATION	FACSIMILE REFERENCES	CONTENTS	NOTES
564	London, BL, Cotton Tiberius B. i	370 / 370.2	191			119r–158r¹⁴	XI med.	Abingdon?		*ASC* C	
565	London, BL, Cotton Tiberius B. i	370 / 370.2	191			158r¹⁵–159v²⁷	XI med.	Abingdon?		continuation	
566	London, BL, Cotton Tiberius B. i	370 / 370.2	191			161r¹⁻²⁷	XI med.	Abingdon?		continuation	
567	London, BL, Cotton Tiberius B. i	370 / 370.2	191			161r²⁷–161v, 163rv	XI med.	Abingdon?		continuation	
568	London, BL, Cotton Tiberius B. i	370 / 370.2	191			160rv, 162r¹⁻⁷	XI med.	Abingdon?		continuation	
569	London, BL, Cotton Tiberius B. i	370 / 370.2	191			162r⁷–162v	XI med.	Abingdon?		continuation	
570	London, BL, Cotton Tiberius B. i	370 / 370.2	191			3r–111v	XI/XII	Abingdon?		frequent minor alterations to Orosius	
571	London, BL, Cotton Tiberius B. iv, fols. 3–9, 19–86	372	192		1	3r–9v	XI med.	Worcester?		chronicle	*ASC* D
572	London, BL, Cotton Tiberius B. iv, fols. 3–9, 19–86	372	192		2	19r–67v	XI med.	Worcester?		chronicle	
573	London, BL, Cotton Tiberius B. iv, fols. 3–9, 19–86	372	192		3	68r–73r, 83r¹¹–86r	XI²	Worcester?		chronicle	
574	London, BL, Cotton Tiberius B. iv, fols. 3–9, 19–86	372	192		4	73v	XI²	Worcester?		chronicle	
575	London, BL, Cotton Tiberius B. iv, fols. 3–9, 19–86	372	192		5	74r–75v²¹	XI med.	Worcester?		chronicle	
576	London, BL, Cotton Tiberius B. iv, fols. 3–9, 19–86	372	192			75v²²–76v³	XI med.	Worcester?		chronicle	
577	London, BL, Cotton Tiberius B. iv, fols. 3–9, 19–86	372	192			76v⁴–77r	XI med.	Worcester?		chronicle	
578	London, BL, Cotton Tiberius B. iv, fols. 3–9, 19–86	372	192			77r–77v	XI med.	Worcester?		chronicle	

HAND NO.	LIBRARY AND SHELF-MARK	GNEUSS	KER	SAWYER/PELTERET	KER HAND NO.	FOLIOS	DATE	LOCATION	FACSIMILE REFERENCES	CONTENTS	NOTES
579	London, BL, Cotton Tiberius B. iv, fols. 3–9, 19–86	372	192			77v–78r	XI med.	Worcester?		chronicle	
580	London, BL, Cotton Tiberius B. iv, fols. 3–9, 19–86	372	192			78r–78r	XI²	Worcester?		chronicle	
580a	London, BL, Cotton Tiberius B. iv, fols. 3–9, 19–86	372	192			78r–78v²	XI²	Worcester?		chronicle	
580b	London, BL, Cotton Tiberius B. iv, fols. 3–9, 19–86	372	192			78v³–78v	XI²	Worcester?		chronicle	
580c	London, BL, Cotton Tiberius B. iv, fols. 3–9, 19–86	372	192			78v–79r	XI²	Worcester?		chronicle	
580d	London, BL, Cotton Tiberius B. iv, fols. 3–9, 19–86	372	192			79r–83r	XI²	Worcester?		chronicle	
◆	London, BL, Cotton Tiberius B. iv, fol. 87rv, *see London, Lambeth Palace Library 1370*										
581	London, BL, Cotton Tiberius B. v, vol. 1, fols. 2–73, 77–88 + London, BL, Cotton Nero D. ii, fols. 238–41	373	193				XI¹/ XI med.	Winchester?	ASMMF 9 EEMF 21	Ælfric, *De temporibus anni, Marvels of the East*, lists, dialogue, pen-trials	margins: *god me helpe* (fol. 19v), *god helpe minum handum* (fol. 28v)
◆	London, BL, Cotton Tiberius B. v, vol. 1, fols. 74 and 76, *see Cambridge, University Library Kk. 1. 24*										
582	London, BL, Cotton Tiberius B. v, vol. 1, fol. 75	374	194			75v	XI¹	Exeter		manumission	name: *wulfgype*
582.5	London, BL, Cotton Tiberius B. xi + Kassel, Gesamthochschulbibliothek 4° Ms. theol. 131	375	195	3		Tib. fols. 1–3, 5, 7; Kassel	890 × 897	Winchester?		Gregory (Alfred), *Regula pastoralis*	fragments
	Oxford, Bodleian Library, Hatton 20		324							King Alfred's preface to Bishop Wærferth's copy of the translation of the *Regula pastoralis*	

HAND NO.	LIBRARY AND SHELF-MARK	GNEUSS	KER	SAWYER/PELTERET	KER HAND NO.	FOLIOS	DATE	LOCATION	FACSIMILE REFERENCES	CONTENTS	NOTES
582.6	London, BL, Cotton Tiberius B. xi + Kassel, Gesamthochschulbibliothek 4° Ms. theol. 131	375	195			Tib. fols. 4, 6, 8	890 × 897			Gregory (Alfred), *Regula pastoralis*	fragments, almost impossible to read
583	London, BL, Cotton Tiberius C. i, fols. 43–203	376	197			109v–111v, 200r–202r	XI² (before 1078)	Sherborne	ASMMF 8	homily, prayer	
584	London, BL, Cotton Tiberius C. i, fols. 43–203	376	197			159v–161v	XI² (before 1078)	Sherborne		prayers, creed, forms of confession	
585	London, BL, Cotton Tiberius C. i, fols. 43–203	376	197			161v–162v	XI² (before 1078)	Sherborne		homily	
585.2	London, BL, Cotton Tiberius C. ii	377	198			5r, 34v, 60v	IX²	Canterbury?		3 short Latin-OE glossaries derived from Bede, *Ecclesiastical History*	
585.4	London, BL, Cotton Tiberius C. ii	377	198			124v	IX²	Canterbury?		a fourth	
585.5	London, BL, Cotton Tiberius C. ii	377	198			5v	X	Canterbury?		explanatory note to Bede, *Ecclesiastical History*	
585.6	London, BL, Cotton Tiberius C. ii	377	198			10v, 73r	X	Canterbury?		2 glosses to Bede, *Ecclesiastical History*	
585.8	London, BL, Cotton Tiberius C. ii	377	198			67r	X	Canterbury?		scribble (between columns of text)	*þe þu me cuðes*
585.8a	London, BL, Cotton Tiberius C. ii	377	198			125r	X	Canterbury?		another (top margin)	*ðrang*
586	London, BL, Cotton Tiberius C. vi	378	199				XI med.	Winchester OM?	ASMMF 2	continous psalter gloss, homily, title	
587	London, BL, Cotton Titus A. iv	379	200		1	2r–50r	XI med.	Canterbury StA? Winchester?	ASMMF 19	bilingual Benedictine Rule	
588	London, BL, Cotton Titus A. iv	379	200		2	51v¹–107r²	XI med.	Canterbury StA? Winchester?		bilingual Benedictine Rule	
589	London, BL, Cotton Titus A. iv	379	200			e.g. 74r	XI med.	Canterbury StA? Winchester?		corrections	

HAND NO.	LIBRARY AND SHELF-MARK	GNEUSS	KER	SAWYER/PELTERET	KER HAND NO.	FOLIOS	DATE	LOCATION	FACSIMILE REFERENCES	CONTENTS	NOTES
590	London, BL, Cotton Titus D. xxvi + xxvii	380	202			D. xxvii. 25v	1023 × 1031	Winchester NM		computistical note	
♦	London, BL, Cotton Titus D. xxvii, *see Cambridge, Trinity College R. 15. 32, pp. 13–36*										
591	*unused number*										
592	London, BL, Cotton Titus D. xxvi + xxvii	380	202			D. xxvi. 2rv	XI¹	Winchester NM		directions for devotion	
593	London, BL, Cotton Titus D. xxvi + xxvii	380	202			D. xxvi. 16v–17r	XI¹	Winchester NM		title, medical recipe	
594	London, BL, Cotton Titus D. xxvi + xxvii	380	202			D. xxvi. 17v–18r	XI¹	Winchester NM		rules of confraternity	
595	London, BL, Cotton Titus D. xxvi + xxvii	380	202			D. xxvii. 55v–56v	XI¹	Winchester NM		prognostics	
596	London, BL, Cotton Titus D. xxvi + xxvii	380	202			D. xxvii. 56v	XI¹	Winchester NM		notes on the sun, the moon and the age of the virgin	
596.8	London, BL, Cotton Vespasian A. i	381	203				IX med.	Canterbury StA?	EEMF 14, ASMMF 2	continuous psalter gloss	
597	London, BL, Cotton Vespasian A. i	381	203			155r¹–156r¹⁰	XI med.	Canterbury CC? StA?		continuous gloss to hymn and creed; plus occasional additional glosses to psalter elsewhere	
597.5	London, BL, Cotton Vespasian A. xiv, fols. 114–79	383	204			153r	XI¹			gloss on decisions of Council of Chelsea	
598	London, BL, Cotton Vespasian B. vi, fols. 1–103	384	205			33r, 39v	XI in.			3 glosses to Bede, *De temporum ratione*	
599	London, BL, Cotton Vespasian B. x, fols. 31–124	386	206			31v, 33v, 34r, 40r	XI in.	Worcester?		4 glosses to Ethicus, *Cosmographia*	
599.4	London, BL, Cotton Vespasian D. vi, fols. 2–77	390	207			2r–66v, 77v	X med.	Canterbury StA?	ASMMF 4	many interlinear glosses to *Parabolae Salomonis* and Alcuin, *De virtutibus et vitiis*; interpretation of Latin names of relationship and other hard words	

HAND NO.	LIBRARY AND SHELF-MARK	GNEUSS	KER	SAWYER/PELTERET	KER HAND NO.	FOLIOS	DATE	LOCATION	FACSIMILE REFERENCES	CONTENTS	NOTES
599.6	London, BL, Cotton Vespasian D. vi, fols. 2–77	390	207			68v–73v	X med.	Canterbury StA?		2 poems ('Kentish Hymn' and Psalm 50); between them, a note on the age of the world	
600	London, BL, Cotton Vespasian D. xii	391	208		1		XI med.	Canterbury CC	ASMMF 4	continuous gloss to hymns and canticles	
◆	London, BL, Cotton Vespasian D. xii, *see London, BL, Cotton Julius A. vi*										
600.4	London, BL, Cotton Vespasian D. xiv, fols. 170–224	392	210			170r	X[1]	Canterbury CC ?	ASMMF 8	2 Latin words glossed in OE	top margin
600.6	London, BL, Cotton Vespasian D. xv, fols. 68–101	393	211			68r	X med.			title to a Latin form of confession	
600.8	London, BL, Cotton Vespasian D. xx, fols. 87–93		212			87r–92v	X[1]			confessional prayer	
◆	London, BL, Cotton Vespasian D. xxii, fols. 18–40, *see Oxford, Bodleian Library, Laud Misc. 509*										
601	London, BL, Cotton Vitellius A. vii, fols. 1–112	397	213			13r–14v	XI[1] (after 1030)	Ramsey		forms of exorcism	
602	London, BL, Cotton Vitellius A. xv, fols. 94–209	399	216		1	94r–175v[3]	X/XI		EEMF 12	St Christopher homily, *Marvels of the East, Letter of Alexander to Aristotle, Beowulf* (to line 1939)	
603	London, BL, Cotton Vitellius A. xv, fols. 94–209	399	216		2	175v[4]–209v	X/XI			rest of *Beowulf, Judith*	
603.7	London, BL, Cotton Vitellius A. xix	401	217				X med.	Canterbury StA?	ASMMF 10	2 glosses to Bede, *Vita S. Cuthberti* (prose)	
603.8	London, BL, Cotton Vitellius A. xix	401	217				X med.	Canterbury StA?		13 glosses to Bede, *Vita S. Cuthberti* (verse)	
604	London, BL, Cotton Vitellius A. xix	401	217			65r	XI			directions to reader	
605	London, BL, Cotton Vitellius C. iii, fols. 11–85	402	219			12r–82v	XI[1]		EEMF 27, ASMMF 1	pharmacopoeia	

HAND NO.	LIBRARY AND SHELF-MARK	GNEUSS	KER	SAWYER/PELTERET	KER HAND NO.	FOLIOS	DATE	LOCATION	FACSIMILE REFERENCES	CONTENTS	NOTES
606	London, BL, Cotton Vitellius C. iii, fols. 11–85	402	219			19v–80v	XI med.			captions to figures	
607	London, BL, Cotton Vitellius C. iii, fols. 11–85	402	219			18va^3–18vb^3	XI^2			2 medical recipes	
608	London, BL, Cotton Vitellius C. iii, fols. 11–85	402	219			80vb^{20}	XI^1			interlinear correction	
609	London, BL, Cotton Vitellius C. iii, fols. 11–85	402	219			82vb^{21}–83ra^{19}	XI med.			2 medical recipes	
610	London, BL, Cotton Vitellius C. iii, fols. 11–85	402	219			83ra^{20}–83ra^{31}	XI ex. or XI/XII			medical recipe	
611	London, BL, Cotton Vitellius C. iii, fols. 11–85	402	219			83rb^1–83rb^{15}	XI ex. or XI/XII			medical recipe	
612	London, BL, Cotton Vitellius C. v	403	220		1		X/XI		ASMMF 17	homilies	main hand of original book
612a	London, BL, Cotton Vitellius C. v	403	220			88v^{21}	X/XI				probably main hand but smaller script
612b	London, BL, Cotton Vitellius C. v	403	220			161v, 162r, 163v, 164r	X/XI				
612c	London, BL, Cotton Vitellius C. v	403	220			192v	X/XI				
613	London, BL, Cotton Vitellius C. v	403	220		2	186$v^{1–6}$, 191$r^{13–26}$	X/XI			homilies	
614	London, BL, Cotton Vitellius C. v	403	220		3	168$v^{1–3}$, 185$r^{33–9}$, 191v^1–192v^{26}	X/XI			homilies	
615	London, BL, Cotton Vitellius C. v	403	220			236v, 239r–254v	X/XI			'appendix'	
616	London, BL, Cotton Vitellius C. v	403	220			1$r^{5–34}$, 4r^1–5v^3, 17v^{17}–21v^{26}, 3r^1–35r^{11}, 69r^1–75v, 95r^1–96r^3, 96$r^{21–30}$, 131r^3–149r^2, 168v^{24}–184v^{36}, 229r^1–231v^{36}	XI^1			'interpolations'	

HAND NO.	LIBRARY AND SHELF-MARK	GNEUSS	KER	SAWYER/PELTERET	KER HAND NO.	FOLIOS	DATE	LOCATION	FACSIMILE REFERENCES	CONTENTS	NOTES
617	London, BL, Cotton Vitellius C. viii, fols. 22–5	404	221			22r–24v	XI[1]		ASMMF 12	instruction for prayer, Egyptian days, Ælfric, *De temporibus anni* (fragment)	
618	London, BL, Cotton Vitellius C. viii, fols. 22–5	404	221			25r[1–10]	XI[1]			computistical notes	
619	London, BL, Cotton Vitellius D. xvii, fols. 4–92	406	222	I		15r–16v, 22r–54r[19]	XI med.		ASMMF 19	saints' lives	manuscript much damaged by fire, leaves disordered
620	London, BL, Cotton Vitellius D. xvii, fols. 4–92	406	222	2		7r–13v, 54r[21]–72v, 92rv	XI med.			saints' lives	
621	London, BL, Cotton Vitellius D. xvii, fols. 4–92	406	222	3		5rv, 17r–21v, 73rv, 77rv, 79r–82v	XI med.			saints' lives	
621a	London, BL, Cotton Vitellius D. xvii, fols. 4–92	406	222	3		4rv, 6rv, 14rv, 74r–76v, 78rv, 83r–91v	XI med.			saints' lives	
622	London, BL, Cotton Vitellius E. xviii	407	224			18r–140v	XI med.	Winchester NM	ASMMF 2	continuous psalter gloss	
622a	London, BL, Cotton Vitellius E. xviii	407	224			9r[1–26], 13r[16–36], 15r[1]–16v[25]	XI med.	Winchester NM		computistical notes, lucky and unlucky days, charms, medical recipes, gloss on diagram notes, riddle with consonant for vowel cipher and explanation of secret writing	
623	London, BL, Cotton Vitellius E. xviii	407	224			2r–7v	XI med.	Winchester NM		names of the months in a Latin calendar	
624	London, BL, Cotton Vitellius E. xviii	407	224			21v	XI med.	Winchester NM		added gloss	
625	London, BL, Cotton Vitellius E. xviii	407	224			139v	XI[2]	Winchester NM		added gloss	
626	London, BL, Harley 55, fols. 1–4	412	225			1r–3r	XI[1]	Worcester or York		recipes	
627	London, BL, Harley 55, fols. 1–4	412	225			3v–4v[1]	XI[1]	Worcester or York		laws of Edgar	

HAND NO.	LIBRARY AND SHELF-MARK	GNEUSS	KER	SAWYER/PELTERET	KER HAND NO.	FOLIOS	DATE	LOCATION	FACSIMILE REFERENCES	CONTENTS	NOTES
628	London, BL, Harley 55, fols. 1–4	412	225			4*v*²	XI¹	Worcester or York		pen trial	
628.5	London, BL, Harley 55, fols. 1–4	412	225			4*v*³	XI¹	Worcester or York		novice copyist's note	names: *ælfmær pattafox, ælfric cild*
629	London, BL, Harley 55, fols. 1–4	412	225	1453		4*v*⁴⁻²²	XI¹	Worcester or York		land memorandum	
◆	London, BL, Harley 55, fols. 1–4, *see Copenhagen, Kongelige Bibliotek G. K. S. 1595*										
630	London, BL, Harley 107	414	227		1	1*r*–7*r*, 8*r*–49*r*²	XI med.	Canterbury StA?	ASMMF 15	Ælfric, *Grammar*	
631	London, BL, Harley 107	414	227		3	7*v*	XI med.	Canterbury StA?		Ælfric, *Grammar*	
632	London, BL, Harley 107	414	227		2	49*r*²–72*v*	XI med.	Canterbury StA?		Ælfric, *Grammar and Glossary*	
633	London, BL, Harley 110	415	228			3*r*–53*r*	X ex.	Canterbury CC		17 glosses to Prosper, *Epigrammata* and *Versus ad coniugem*, Isidore, *Synonyma*	
634	London, BL, Harley 110	415	228			27*r*	XI	Canterbury CC		1 further gloss to Isidore	
635	London, BL, Harley 208	417	229			88*r*	X/XI	York		OE words and alphabet containing OE special characters in lower margin	OE verse line (cf. *Beowulf* 869): *hwæt ic eall feala ealde sæge*
636	London, BL, Harley 526, fols. 1–27	419	230				X/XI?		ASMMF 10	15 glosses to Bede, *Vita S. Cuthberti*	
637	London, BL, Harley 526, fols. 1–27	419	230			2*r*	X/XI?			name in margin	*ælfric wulfrices* (son? of Wulfric)
638	London, BL, Harley 585	421	231			1*r*–114*v*, 130*r*–179*r*¹⁰	X/XI		ASMMF 1	herbal	
639	London, BL, Harley 585	421	231			115*r*–129*v*	XI¹			herbal	
640	London, BL, Harley 585	421	231			179*r*¹¹–190*v*	XI¹			herbal	

HAND NO.	LIBRARY AND SHELF-MARK	GNEUSS	KER	SAWYER/PELTERET	KER HAND NO.	FOLIOS	DATE	LOCATION	FACSIMILE REFERENCES	CONTENTS	NOTES
641	London, BL, Harley 585	421	231			191r–193r	XI^1			herbal	
642	London, BL, Harley 863	425	232			107rv	XI 3rd ¼	Exeter	ASMMF 4	continuous gloss to canticle	
643	London, BL, Harley 1117	427	234			45v–62r	X/XI or XI^1	Canterbury CC?	ASMMF 10	47 glosses to Bede, *Vita S. Cuthberti*	
644	London, BL, Harley 2110, fols. 4*, 5*	428	235				XI^1		ASMMF 8	fragments of homilies	
644.5	London, BL, Harley 2965	432	237	1560		40v	IX/X		ASMMF 1	bounds	
645	London, BL, Harley 3271	435	239			6v^1–6v^{22}	XI^1		ASMMF 15	tribal hidage	
646	London, BL, Harley 3271	435	239			7r^1–52r^{27}, 79v^{23}–90r^{20}	XI^1			Ælfric, *Grammar*	
647	London, BL, Harley 3271	435	239			53r^1–79v^{23}	XI^1			Ælfric, *Grammar*	
648	London, BL, Harley 3271	435	239			90r^{21}–90v^{17}, 92v^{24-31}, 125v^1–129r^{22}	XI^1			notes on the 30 pieces of silver, on Noah's ark, on Solomon's gold and on the 6 ages of the world, excerpts from Ælfric, *Letter to Sigeweard*	
649	London, BL, Harley 3271	435	239			90v^{20}–91r^7	XI^1			*De diebus malis* (part)	
650	London, BL, Harley 3271	435	239			91r^8–91r^{24}	XI^1			*De diebus malis* (part)	
651	London, BL, Harley 3271	435	239			91r^{25}–91v^{29}	XI^1			menologium, computistical notes	
652	London, BL, Harley 3271	435	239			92r^1–92v^{13}	XI^1			computistical notes	
653	London, BL, Harley 3271	435	239			92v^{14}–92v^{23}	XI^1			computistical notes	
654	London, BL, Harley 3271	435	239			115v–118r^{23}	XI^1			Abbo of Saint-Germain, *Bella Parisiacae urbis*	
655	London, BL, Harley 3271	435	239			120v, 121v, 123v	XI^1			2 glosses to prognostics, 1 gloss in glossary	
656	London, BL, Harley 3271	435	239			124r^{10}–125r^{27}	XI^1			Ælfric homily	
657	London, BL, Harley 3376 + Oxford, Bodleian Library, Lat.misc.a.3, fol. 49 + Lawrence, Univ. of Kansas, Spencer Research Library, Pryce P.2.A	436	240S				X/XI		ASMMF 7	Lat.–OE glossary	fragments
658	London, BL, Harley 3826	438	241				X/XI	Abingdon?	ASMMF 15	2 glosses	

HAND NO.	LIBRARY AND SHELF-MARK	GNEUSS	KER	SAWYER/PELTERET	KER HAND NO.	FOLIOS	DATE	LOCATION	FACSIMILE REFERENCES	CONTENTS	NOTES
659	London, BL, Harley 5915, fols. 8–9 + Bloomington, Indiana University, Lilly Library, Add. 1000	441	242 384S				XI¹		ASMMF 16	Ælfric, *Grammar*	fragments
660	London, BL, Harley 5915, fol. 13 + Cambridge, Magdalene College, Pepys 2981, no. 16	442	243				XI in.		ASMMF 16	homilies	
661	London, BL, Harley 7653	443	244				X/XI?	Worcester?	ASMMF 1	gloss to prayer	owner female?
662	London, BL, Harley Charter 43 C 1			376			X² or XI	Winchester OM?		bounds	
663	London, BL, Harley Charter 43 C 2			697	I*rv*		X²	Winchester OM?		bounds and endorsement	
◆	London, BL, Harley Charter 43 C 3, *see London, BL, Cotton Charter viii 28*										
664	London, BL, Harley Charter 43 C 4			1494 1486	I*r*¹–I*r*¹⁸ I*r*¹⁹–I*v*¹¹		X/XI			wills	
665	London, BL, Harley Charter 43 C 4			1486	I*v*¹¹⁻¹⁹		XI¹			bounds	
666	London, BL, Harley Charter 43 C 5			738			X²			bounds	
667	London, BL, Harley Charter 43 C 6			801			X² or XI¹			bounds	
668	London, BL, Harley Charter 43 C 7			1379			995			bounds	
◆	London, BL, Harley Charter 43 C 8, *see London, BL, Cotton Charter viii 9*										
668.5	London, BL, Harley Charter 83 A 1			173			IX¹			endorsement	
669	London, BL, Harley Charter 83 A 2			1534	I*r*		1000 × 1001			will	
669.1	London, BL, Harley Charter 83 A 2			1534	I*v*		XI			endorsement	
◆	London, BL, Harley Charter 83 A 3, *see Cambridge, Corpus Christi Coll. 391*										
669.5	London, BL, Royal 1 B. VII	445	246		I5*v*		X¹ (soon after 924)		ASMMF 7	manumission	

Hand no.	Library and shelf-mark	Gneuss	Ker	Sawyer/Pelteret	Ker hand no.	Folios	Date	Location	Facsimile references	Contents	Notes
670	London, BL, Royal 1 D. IX	447	247			43v¹⁻⁴	XI¹	Canterbury CC	ASMMF 7	notice of confraternity	
◆	London, BL, Royal 1 D. IX, *see London, BL, Cotton Claudius A. iii, fols. 4–6*										
671	London, BL, Royal 2 A. XX	450	248			5r, 8r, 10rv, 11v–15r, 19r, 22r, 24r, 29r–38r, 39r, 44r, 45v, 50r	X¹	Worcester?	ASMMF 1	glosses to paternoster, creed, etc.; 23 titles to prayers; notes ascribing each clause of the creed to an apostle; note on moonrise; scribbles (?) in margins	
671.5	London, BL, Royal 2 B. V	451	249				X med.	Winchester?	ASMMF 2	continuous gloss to psalter	
672	London, BL, Royal 2 B. V	451	249	2		190v⁸–196v⁹	X/XI	Canterbury CC?		2 prayers	
673	London, BL, Royal 2 B. V	451	249	3		196v	XI¹	Canterbury CC		notice of fasting days	
674	London, BL, Royal 2 B. V	451	249	4		197r¹–198r¹⁹	XI¹	Canterbury CC		prayers	
675	London, BL, Royal 2 B. V	451	249			190v⁸–196v⁹	XI¹	Canterbury CC		alterations to prayers	
676	London, BL, Royal 2 B. V	451	249			19v, 41r, 50rv, 55v, 60rv, 61v, 63v, 64r, 80v, 85v, 86r, 107v, 145r, 153v	XI¹			glosses added in margins and occasionally between lines	
677	London, BL, Royal 2 B. V	451	249	5		6r¹⁴⁻²⁰	XI med.	Winchester or Canterbury . CC?		2 maxims and 2 proverbs	
678	London, BL, Royal 2 B. V	451	249	6		6va¹⁻⁴⁹, 6vb¹⁻²³	XI med.	Winchester or Canterbury CC?		prayer	
679	London, BL, Royal 2 B. V	451	249			1r	XI med.			4 glosses to Latin words	margin
680	London, BL, Royal 2 B. V	451	249			198v	XI ex.	Canterbury CC		personal note	desire to return to Christ Church for Christmas

HAND NO.	LIBRARY AND SHELF-MARK	GNEUSS	KER	SAWYER/PELTÉRET	KER HAND NO.	FOLIOS	DATE	LOCATION	FACSIMILE REFERENCES	CONTENTS	NOTES
681	London, BL, Royal 2 B. V	451	249			198v	XI ex.	Canterbury CC		note (charter?)	mentions 'Lady' and 'King'
682	London, BL, Royal 2 B. V	451	249			198v	XI ex.	Canterbury CC		scribble	*gyrnað embe gretað gramm*
682.5	London, BL, Royal 4 A. XIV, fols. 107–8	456	251			107r	VIII/IX		ASMMF 4	1 gloss to *Vita S. Guthlaci*	
683	London, BL, Royal 5 E. XI	458	252	Ia		10v13, 10v16, etc.	XI1	Canterbury CC	ASMMF 4	many glosses to Aldhelm, *De virginitate*	tall ascenders
684	London, BL, Royal 5 E. XI	458	252	Ia		10v etc.	XI1	Canterbury CC		further glosses	darker ink, upright *d*, insular *g*
685	London, BL, Royal 5 E. XI	458	252	Ia		22r9, 22r10–11, 22v15	XI1	Canterbury CC		further glosses	small clear script
686	London, BL, Royal 5 E. XI	458	252	Ia		30r12, 37r6	XI1	Canterbury CC		further glosses	larger script
687	London, BL, Royal 5 E. XI	458	252	Ia		13v, 28v15	XI1	Canterbury CC		further glosses	paler ink
688	London, BL, Royal 5 E. XI	458	252	Ia		41v11 etc.	XI1	Canterbury CC		further glosses	very small
689	London, BL, Royal 5 E. XI	458	252	Ia		44r5 etc.	XI1	Canterbury CC		further glosses	margin
690	London, BL, Royal 5 E. XI	458	252	Ia		71r	XI1	Canterbury CC		1 gloss	margin
691	London, BL, Royal 5 E. XI	458	252	Ia		91r7	XI1	Canterbury CC		1 gloss	margin
692	London, BL, Royal 5 E. XI	458	252	Ib		116r–117v	XI1	Canterbury CC		6 glosses	
693	London, BL, Royal 5 E. XI	458	252	Ic		13r, 17r–20r	XI med.	Canterbury CC		later glosses in larger script	
694	London, BL, Royal 5 E. XI	458	252	Ic		70v, 82v–84r	XI med.	Canterbury CC		further glosses	

HAND NO.	LIBRARY AND SHELF-MARK	GNEUSS	KER	SAWYER/PELTERET	KER HAND NO.	FOLIOS	DATE	LOCATION	FACSIMILE REFERENCES	CONTENTS	NOTES
695	London, BL, Royal 5 E. XI	458	252		1c	117*v*, 118*v*	XI med.	Canterbury CC		further glosses	
696	London, BL, Royal 5 E. XI	458	252			13*r*$^{16-19}$	XI	Canterbury CC		additional glosses	margin
697	London, BL, Royal 5 E. XI	458	252			20*r*^{10}	XI¹	Canterbury CC		1 gloss	
698	London, BL, Royal 5 E. XI	458	252			89*v*	XI¹	Canterbury CC		English alphabet interlined as syntactic markers	
699	London, BL, Royal 5 F. III	462	253			2*v*, 3*r*	XI in.	Worcester?	ASMMF 4	18 glosses to Aldhelm, *De virginitate*	
700	London, BL, Royal 5 F. III	462	253			15*r*	XI¹	Worcester?		1 later gloss	margin
701	London, BL, Royal 5 F. III	462	253			1*r*, 17*r*	XI¹	Worcester?		names	margin: *hacun*; *hacun eor*
702	London, BL, Royal 5 F. III	462	253			7*r*	X²	Worcester?		partial text (writ?)	margin; includes name: *Godwine mun*
703	London, BL, Royal 5 F. III	462	253			8*r*	XI²?	Worcester?		partial text	margin: *æðer ge weras ge wuif ða ða he*
704	London, BL, Royal 6 A. VI	464	254				XI¹	Canterbury CC	ASMMF 23	glosses to Aldhelm, *De virginitate*	
705	London, BL, Royal 6 A. VI	464	254			42*v*–46*r*	XI¹	Canterbury CC		further glosses	
706	London, BL, Royal 6 B. VII	466	255				XI²	Exeter		glosses to Aldhelm, *De virginitate*	
707	London, BL, Royal 7 C. IV	470	256				XI med.	Canterbury CC	ASMMF 5	glosses to Defensor of Ligugé, *Liber scintillarum*	
708	London, BL, Royal 7 C. IV	470	256			24*rv*, 31*rv*, 25*rv*	XI med.	Canterbury CC		further glosses	
709	London, BL, Royal 7 C. XII	472	257		1	4*r*–25*r*, 46*r*–90*v*	X ex.	Cerne, Dorset	EEMF 13, ASMMF 17	homilies	

HAND NO.	LIBRARY AND SHELF-MARK	GNEUSS	KER	SAWYER/PELTERET	KER HAND NO.	FOLIOS	DATE	LOCATION	FACSIMILE REFERENCES	CONTENTS	NOTES
710	London, BL, Royal 7 C. XII	472	257		2	$25v$–$45v$, $91r$–$218r$	X ex.	Cerne, Dorset		homilies (cont.)	also many corrections to the work of Hand 1
711	London, BL, Royal 7 C. XII	472	257			$197v^{1-5}$	X ex.	Cerne, Dorset		homily (cont.)	new hand
712	London, BL, Royal 7 C. XII	472	257			$64r$, $76r^{25}$, $105r$	X ex.	Cerne, Dorset		margin and page foot	hand of Ælfric of Eynsham
712a	London, BL, Royal 7 C. XII	472	257			$97r^{24}$, $106v^4$, $132v^{16}$, $133v^2$ and 25, $134r^{14}$, $167v^1$, $170v^{15}$ (first few words in margin), $212r^5$, $213v^6$	X ex.	Cerne, Dorset		alterations and additions, probably also $189v^{14}$	hand similar to Ælfric's
712b	London, BL, Royal 7 C. XII	472	257			$131v^{4-5}$	X ex.	Cerne, Dorset		additions	very like Ælfric's hand but one very unusual spelling, *þarrihte*
712c	London, BL, Royal 7 C. XII	472	257			$164v$	X ex.	Cerne, Dorset		additional text	inserted part leaf
713	London, BL, Royal 7 C. XII	472	257			$170v^{15}$	X ex.	Cerne, Dorset		last 7 words in margin	
714	London, BL, Royal 7 C. XII	472	257			$66r^{11}$, $71v^{11}$, $71v^{13}$, $78v^1$, $88r^1$, $96v^{11}$, $99r^7$, $131v^{14}$, $133r^7$	X ex.	Cerne, Dorset		alterations and additions	
715	London, BL, Royal 7 C. XII	472	257			$169r^{1-9}$	X ex.	Cerne, Dorset		additional text	inserted part leaf
715.1	London, BL, Royal 7 C. XII	472	257			$169r^9$	X ex.	Cerne, Dorset		1 added word	*iohanne*
716	London, BL, Royal 7 C. XII	472	257			$20r^{15}$, $22r^7$, $31r^{20}$, $35r^{18}$, $111r^5$, $123v^{20}$, $147r^{2-3}$, $151r^5$, $157v^{11, 21}$, $210v^{10}$	X ex.	Cerne, Dorset		alterations and additions; perhaps also $9r^{13}$, $124r^9$	
717	London, BL, Royal 7 C. XII	472	257			$13v^{11}$, $29r^{21}$, $49r^2$, $50r^{16}$, $77r^7$, $141r^2$, $141v^{20}$, $198r^{12}$	X ex.	Cerne, Dorset		alterations and additions	
718	London, BL, Royal 7 C. XII	472	257			$143r^2$	X/XI			addition, cf. also $176v^{21}$	
719	London, BL, Royal 7 C. XII	472	257			$153r^{5, 10}$	X/XI			alterations	
720	London, BL, Royal 7 C. XII	472	257			$9v^{16}$, $10r^9$, $12v^6$	XI			alterations and additions	

HAND NO.	LIBRARY AND SHELF-MARK	GNEUSS	KER	SAWYER/PELTERET	KER HAND NO.	FOLIOS	DATE	LOCATION	FACSIMILE REFERENCES	CONTENTS	NOTES
721	London, BL, Royal 7 C. XII	472	257			141r^1	XI			superscript addition	
722	London, BL, Royal 7 C. XII	472	257			124v	XI ex.			addition	lower margin
723	London, BL, Royal 7 C. XII	472	257			80v–82r	XI/XII			alterations and glosses	
724	London, BL, Royal 7 C. XII	472	257			190r^{14}	XI			margin	name: *ælfstan*
724.2	London, BL, Royal 7 D. XXIV, fols. 82–168	473	259			86v^{26}, 87$r^{2, 23 (2), 26}$, 94r^{24}, 95$r^{10, 14, 21 (2)}$, 99$r^{6, 12, 22}$, 104v^9, 115v^{23}, 119v^{15}, 122r^1, 134r^4	X med.	Glastonbury?	ASMMF 23	18 glosses to Aldhelm, *De virginitate*	high *d*, straight *y*
724.3	London, BL, Royal 7 D. XXIV, fols. 82–168	473	259			95r^{18}, 96v^7, 103v^{23}, 104r^{12}, 119v^{15}, 122$v^{5, 10}$, 136v^7, 149v^{23}, 151$r^{5, 10, 20}$, 151v^{26}, 152r^{11}, 158v^{23}				15 further glosses in tiny writing	
724.4	London, BL, Royal 7 D. XXIV, fols. 82–168	473	259			87$r^{6, 24}$, 87$v^{1, 19}$				4 further glosses	low *d*, open *g*, occasional open *e*
724.5	London, BL, Royal 7 D. XXIV, fols. 82–168	473	259			87$v^{11, 12}$	X med.			2 further glosses	very faint
724.6	London, BL, Royal 7 D. XXIV, fols. 82–168	473	259			123v^8, 124r^{14}	X			2 further glosses	large, bold
724.7	London, BL, Royal 7 D. XXIV, fols. 82–168	473	259			88$r^{19 (2)}$				2 further glosses	in right margin
725	London, BL, Royal 8 C. VII, fols. 1, 2	476	260				XI in.		ASMMF 19	lives of saints	fragment
726	London, BL, Royal 12 C. XXIII	478	263				X/XI	Canterbury CC		1 gloss to Julian of Toledo, *Prognost. fut. saec.*, 27 to Aldhelm, *Ænigmata*	
727	London, BL, Royal 12 C. XXIII	478	263				XI^1	Canterbury CC		48 further glosses to Aldhelm	
727.5	London, BL, Royal 12 D. XVII	479	264			49r	XI		ASMMF 1	medical recipe	

HAND NO.	LIBRARY AND SHELF-MARK	GNEUSS	KER	SAWYER/PELTERET	KER HAND NO.	FOLIOS	DATE	LOCATION	FACSIMILE REFERENCES	CONTENTS	NOTES
◆	London, BL, Royal 12 D. XVII, *see Cambridge, Corpus Christi Coll. 173, fols. 1–56*										
728	London, BL, Royal 12 G. XII, fols. 2–9 + Oxford, All Souls College 38, fols. 1–12	480	265	1		Royal 7*r*–8*v*; Oxf. 1*r*–12*v*	XI med.		ASMMF 15	Ælfric, *Grammar*	fragments
729	London, BL, Royal 12 G. XII, fols. 2–9 + Oxford, All Souls College 38, fols. 1–12	480	265	2		Royal 2*r*–6*v*, 9*rv*	XI med.			further fragments	
730	London, BL, Royal 13 A. XV	484	266				XI[1]	Worcester?	ASMMF 19	glosses to Felix, *Vita S. Guthlaci*	
731	London, BL, Royal 15 A. XVI	489	267			73*r*[20]	X/XI	Canterbury StA	ASMMF 19	1 gloss to Aldhelm, *Ænigmata*	
732	London, BL, Royal 15 A. XVI	489	267			76*v*[16]	X/XI	Canterbury StA		1 gloss to *Scholica Graecarum glossarum*	
733	London, BL, Royal 15 B. XIX, fols. 1–35	491	268			3*r*, 5*r*, 6*r*, 16*v*, 28*r*, 30*r*	XI[1]	Canterbury CC		glosses to Sedulius, *Carmen paschale*	
734	London, BL, Royal 15 B. XXII	494	269				XI[2]		ASMMF 15	Ælfric, *Grammar*	
735	London, BL, Royal 15 C. VII	496	270			109*r*, 111*r*	XI[1]	Winchester OM	ASMMF 19	glosses to Wulfstan the Cantor, *Narratio metrica de S. Swithuno*	
◆	London, BL, Stowe 2, *see Cambridge, University Library Ii. 4. 6*										
736	London, BL, Stowe 2	499	271			57*r*, 100*r*, 101*r*[1]	XI med.	Winchester NM	ASMMF 2	additional glosses to continuous psalter gloss	
◆	London, BL, Stowe 944, *see Cambridge, Trinity College R. 15. 32, pp. 13–36*										
737	London, BL, Stowe 944	500	274			28*v*b[8]	XI[1]	Winchester NM	EEMF 26	additional name to *Liber vitae* with words in English	*godwine iustines sunu*
738	London, BL, Stowe 944	500	274			28*v* top margin	XI[2]	Winchester NM		additional name to *Liber vitae* with words in English	*leofred . . .*
739	London, BL, Stowe 944	500	274			29*ra*[27]	XI[2]	Winchester NM		additional names to *Liber vitae* with phrases in English	*ealdred alfuuoldes sunu . . .*

HAND NO.	LIBRARY AND SHELF-MARK	GNEUSS	KER	SAWYER/PELTERET	KER HAND NO.	FOLIOS	DATE	LOCATION	FACSIMILE REFERENCES	CONTENTS	NOTES
740	London, BL, Stowe 944	500	274			$29r$ top margin	XI²	Winchester NM		additional name to *Liber vitae* in English	*ordgiuu þeo nunne* in red
740.5	London, BL, Stowe 944			1443		$57r$–v	XI¹			incomplete charter	
741	London, BL, Stowe 944	500	274			$58r^{1-2}$, $58r^{14-15}$	XI med.	Winchester NM		heading to list of relics, 1 item in list	
742	London, BL, Stowe 944	500	274			$58r^{23}$–$58v^{13}$	XI med.	Winchester NM		list of relics	
743	London, BL, Stowe 944	500	274			$58v^{14}$–$58v^{24}$	XI med.	Winchester NM		list of relics	
744	London, BL, Stowe 944	500	274			$59v^{26}$–$60r^{25}$	XI med.	Winchester NM		Pseudo-Damasus and Pseudo-Jerome, *Colloquy on the Mass*	
744.3	London, BL, Stowe Charter 1			19			VII/VIII			endorsement	
744.4	London, BL, Stowe Charter 2			22			XI¹				
744.6	London, BL, Stowe Charter 4			111			X²			endorsement	
744.7	London, BL, Stowe Charter 5			123			IX?			phrases in bounds	
745	London, BL, Stowe Charter 6			125			XI med. or XI²			English elements	
745a	London, BL, Stowe Charter 6			125			XI med. or XI²			witness list with English names	
745.1	London, BL, Stowe Charter 7			155			XI			endorsement	
745.2	London, BL, Stowe Charter 8			1500			IX¹			will in English	
745.3	London, BL, Stowe Charter 9			161			XI			endorsement	
745.4	London, BL, Stowe Charter 11			175			X			bounds	see also 409.8
745.5	London, BL, Stowe Charter 12			178			IX			endorsement	
745.6	London, BL, Stowe Charter 13			1266			IX?			endorsement	
745.7	London, BL, Stowe Charter 14			1434			IX¹			bounds	
745.8	London, BL, Stowe Charter 15			1436			IX¹			bounds	
745.9	London, BL, Stowe Charter 16			1269			IX med.			endorsement	

HAND NO.	LIBRARY AND SHELF-MARK	GNEUSS	KER	SAWYER/PELTERET	KER HAND NO.	FOLIOS	DATE	LOCATION	FACSIMILE REFERENCES	CONTENTS	NOTES
745.10	London, BL, Stowe Charter 17		293				XI			bounds	
745.11	London, BL, Stowe Charter 17		293				XI			endorsement	
◆	London, BL, Stowe Charter 19, *see Canterbury, Cathedral Library, Chart. Ant. M. 14*										
745.12	London, BL, Stowe Charter 19		344		I*v*		IX/X ?			endorsement	
745.13	London, BL, Stowe Charter 20		1508				IX²			will in English	
745.14	London, BL, Stowe Charter 20		1508				IX²			endorsement	
745.15	London, BL, Stowe Charter 22		367				X			bounds	
◆	London, BL, Stowe Charter 24, *see London, BL, Cotton Augustus ii 23*										
745.16	London, BL, Stowe Charter 24		512				X			endorsement	
◆	London, BL, Stowe Charter 25, *see London, BL, Cotton Augustus ii 44*										
745.17	London, BL, Stowe Charter 25		497				X²			endorsement	
◆	London, BL, Stowe Charter 26, *see London, BL, Cotton Augustus ii 44*										
745.18	London, BL, Stowe Charter 27		1506				X med.			agreements in English	
745.19	London, BL, Stowe Charter 28		1211				X med.			charter in English	
◆	London, BL, Stowe Charter 29, *see London, BL, Cotton Charter viii 28*										
746	London, BL, Stowe Charter 29		717		I*v*		X²	Canterbury CC		endorsement	
747	London, BL, Stowe Charter 30		1215				968			bilingual charter	
748	London, BL, Stowe Charter 30		1215		I*r*		X²			addition within witness list and below	
749	London, BL, Stowe Charter 30		1215		I*v*		X²			endorsement	
750	London, BL, Stowe Charter 31		779				XI/XII ?			bilingual charter	

HAND NO.	LIBRARY AND SHELF-MARK	GNEUSS	KER	SAWYER/PELTERET	KER HAND NO.	FOLIOS	DATE	LOCATION	FACSIMILE REFERENCES	CONTENTS	NOTES
751	London, BL, Stowe Charter 32			1451	Ir^{19-24}		972 × 978			bounds	
752	London, BL, Stowe Charter 33			1450			X²			bounds	
753	London, BL, Stowe Charter 34			890	Ir^{14-18}		997	Crediton		bounds	
	Oxford, Bodleian Library, Eng. hist. a. 2, XIII			1492	Ir		1008 × 1012			will	
754	London, BL, Stowe Charter 34			890	Iv^{1-2}		XI	Exeter		endorsement	
755	London, BL, Stowe Charter 35			905	Ir^{7-13}		1002	Canterbury CC		bounds	
756	London, BL, Stowe Charter 36			1487	Ir^{1-14}		975 × 1016			will	
757	London, BL, Stowe Charter 36			1487	Iv^{1-2}		X/XI			endorsement	
758	London, BL, Stowe Charter 36			1487	Iv^{foot}		X/XI			title	
759	London, BL, Stowe Charter 37			1503	Ir^{1-6}		1014			will (part)	
760	London, BL, Stowe Charter 37			1503	Ir^{7-28}		1014			will (conclusion)	
◆	London, BL, Stowe Charter 38, *see London, BL, Cotton Claudius A. iii, fols. 4–6*										
761	London, BL, Stowe Charter 40			981			XI¹?			charter in Latin and English	
762	London, BL, Stowe Charter 41			974	Ir^{9-13}		1035			bounds	
763	London, BL, Stowe Charter 42			1400	Ir^{1-6}		1038 × 1050			charter in English	
763.5	London, College of Arms, Waiting Room			1026			XI/XII			forgery	
764	London, Corporation of London Records Office, Ch. 1a			P 8			1067			writ	
765	London, Corporation of London Records Office, Ch. 2			P 23			XI²			writ	
766	London, Lambeth Palace Library 149, fols. 1–138	506	275			138r	XI¹			4-word note (opening of a writ?)	names: *æþel*, *æþelwerd*

HAND NO.	LIBRARY AND SHELF-MARK	GNEUSS	KER	SAWYER/PELTERET	KER HAND NO.	FOLIOS	DATE	LOCATION	FACSIMILE REFERENCES	CONTENTS	NOTES
767	London, Lambeth Palace Library 173, fols. 157–221	508	276			212v, 214r	XI² or XI/ XII			glosses to extract from Bede, *Historia*	
768	London, Lambeth Palace Library 204	510	277			70v	XI¹	Canterbury CC?		1 gloss to Gregory, *Dialogi*	
769	London, Lambeth Palace Library 204	510	277			25r, 38v, 74v	XI med.	Canterbury CC?		3 more glosses to Gregory, *Dialogi*	
770	London, Lambeth Palace Library 204	510	277			119v, 128v	XI med.	Canterbury CC?		glosses to Ephrem Syrus, *De compunctione cordis*	
771	London, Lambeth Palace Library 204	510	277			129v	XI med.	Canterbury CC?		historical note (part)	includes the name: *œadgares cininges*
772	London, Lambeth Palace Library 237, fols. 146–208	512	278			162v	XI	Glastonbury? Worcester?		pen trial	*writ þus*
772.5	London, Lambeth Palace Library 377	515	279			14r⁶, 18r¹⁶, 39v²	X med.		ASMMF 21	glosses to Isidore	
773	London, Lambeth Palace Library 377	515	279			87r	XI¹			note	*þus scealan preostan*
774	London, Lambeth Palace Library 427, fols. 1–202	517	280			5r¹–183v	XI¹	Winchester?		continuous gloss to psalms	
774a	London, Lambeth Palace Library 427, fols. 1–202	517	280			184r–202v¹⁶	XI¹	Winchester?		continuous gloss to Canticles	
775	London, Lambeth Palace Library 427, fols. 1–202	517	280			5r¹–183v	XI¹	Winchester?		alterations and additions to gloss	
776	London, Lambeth Palace Library 427, fols. 1–202	517	280			141r–142r	XI¹	Winchester?		gloss to prayer	
777	London, Lambeth Palace Library 427, fols. 1–202	517	280			183v⁸⁻¹⁷	XI²	Winchester?		prayer	
778	London, Lambeth Palace Library 427, fols. 210–11	518	281				XI²	Exeter?		history of Kentish royal saints (fragment)	

HAND NO.	LIBRARY AND SHELF-MARK	GNEUSS	KER	SAWYER/PELTERET	KER HAND NO.	FOLIOS	DATE	LOCATION	FACSIMILE REFERENCES	CONTENTS	NOTES
◆	London, Lambeth Palace Library 489, *see London, BL, Cotton Cleopatra B. xiii, fols. 1–58*										
779	London, Lambeth Palace Library 1370 + London, BL, Cotton Tiberius B. iv, fol. 87	521	284S	1		Lamb. 69*v*	XI¹	Canterbury CC		record of consecration	
780	London, Lambeth Palace Library 1370 + London, BL, Cotton Tiberius B. iv, fol. 87	521	284S	2		Lamb. 114*r*	XI¹	Canterbury CC		bounds	
781	London, Lambeth Palace Library 1370 + London, BL, Cotton Tiberius B. iv, fol. 87	521	284S	3		Lamb. 114*r*, 115*r*	XI med.	Canterbury CC		2 records of agreements	
782	London, Lambeth Palace Library 1370 + London, BL, Cotton Tiberius B. iv, fol. 87	521	284S	4		Lamb. 114*v*; Tib. 87*rv*	XI¹	Canterbury CC		3 writs of Cnut	
783	London, The National Archives (PRO) 30/26/11			795			974			bounds	
784	London, Wellcome Historical Medical Lib. 46	523	98S	1		1*r*¹⁻⁵	X/XI		ASMMF 9	recipe	
785	London, Wellcome Historical Medical Lib. 46	523	98S	2		1*r*⁶⁻⁸, 1*r*¹⁶⁻²⁴	X/XI			recipes	
786	London, Wellcome Historical Medical Lib. 46	523	98S	3		1*r*⁹⁻¹⁵	X/XI			recipe	
787	London, Westminster Abbey Muniments 67209	524.2					XI¹		*ASE* 25	homiletic fragment	
788	London, Westminster Abbey Muniments I			1248			XI²			bounds	
788.2	London, Westminster Abbey Muniments II			124		1*r*⁸⁻¹²	XI?			bounds	forgery
788.3	London, Westminster Abbey Muniments II			124		1*v*	XI			endorsement	

HAND NO.	LIBRARY AND SHELF-MARK	GNEUSS	KER	SAWYER/PELTERET	KER HAND NO.	FOLIOS	DATE	LOCATION	FACSIMILE REFERENCES	CONTENTS	NOTES
789	London, Westminster Abbey Muniments V			670			X ex.			bounds	
790	London, Westminster Abbey Muniments VII			753			X² ?			bounds	
791	London, Westminster Abbey Muniments VIII			1447			X²			record of land dispute	
792	London, Westminster Abbey Muniments X			702			X ex.			bounds	
793	London, Westminster Abbey Muniments XII			1140		$1r^{1-10}$	1065 × 1066			writ	
794	London, Westminster Abbey Muniments XV			1145		$1r^{1-6}$	XI²			writ	
795	London, Westminster Abbey Muniments XVI			1142			XI/XII ?			writ	
796	London, Westminster Abbey Muniments XVIII			1125		$1r^{1-6}$	XI/XII ?			writ	
797	London, Westminster Abbey Muniments XIX			1126		$1r^{1-7}$	XI²			writ	
797.3	Longleat House, Wilts, Library of the Marquess of Bath NMR 10564			236			X ?			bounds	
797.4	Longleat House, Wilts, Library of the Marquess of Bath NMR 10565			563			X med.			bounds	
797.5	Los Angeles, Private Collector						X²			gospel fragments	
797.6	Louvain-la-Neuve, Archives de l'Université Catholique de Louvain, Fragmenta H. Omont 3	848	417			$1r$	IX ex. or X in.		ASMMF 13	medical recipes	single page fragment
797.7	Louvain-la-Neuve, Archives de l'Université Catholique de Louvain, Fragmenta H. Omont 3	848	417			$1v$	XI in.			4-word beginning of a prayer	
797.8	Marburg, Hessisches Staatarchiv, 319 Pfarrei Spangenberg Hr Nr. 1	849.6	421				VIII¹		ASMMF 9	1 gloss (*fetherhaman*) on Servius, *In Aeneida*	2-leaf fragment

HAND NO.	LIBRARY AND SHELF-MARK	GNEUSS	KER	SAWYER/PELTERET	KER HAND NO.	FOLIOS	DATE	LOCATION	FACSIMILE REFERENCES	CONTENTS	NOTES
798	Munich, Bayerische Staatsbibliothek clm 29336 (1	852	286				XI¹			2 glosses to Prudentius, *Psychomachia*	
◆	New Haven, Yale Univ., Beinecke Lib. 401 and 401A, *see Cambridge, University Library Add. 3330*										
799	New Haven, Yale Univ., Beinecke Lib. 578	859	1				X/XI or XI¹	Canterbury?		gospel fragments	
799.1	New Haven, Yale Univ., Beinecke Lib. 578	859	1				X/XI or XI¹	Canterbury?		rubric to gospel reading	
◆	New Haven, Yale Univ., Beinecke Lib., Osborn fa 26, *see Cambridge, Queen's College, (Horne) 75*										
800	New York, Pierpont Morgan Lib. G 63	866	418S				XI²			Exodus fragments	
800.8	New York, Pierpont Morgan Lib. M 776	862	287				IX			glosses to psalter	
801	New York, Pierpont Morgan Lib. M 776	862	287				X²			glosses to psalter	
◆	Oslo and London, The Schøyen Collection 197, *see Cambridge, University Library Add. 3330*										
802	Oslo and London, The Schøyen Collection 600			1220			999 × 1020			charter in English	offered for sale at Sotherby's 10 July 2012, lot 37
◆	Oxford, All Souls College 38, *see London, BL, Royal 12 G. XII*										
803	Oxford, Bodleian Library, Ashmole 328	526	288				XI med.	Canterbury CC?		Byrhtferth, *Enchiridion*	
803a	Oxford, Bodleian Library, Ashmole 328	526	288			pp. 245–6	XI med.	Canterbury CC?		titles	

HAND NO.	LIBRARY AND SHELF-MARK	GNEUSS	KER	SAWYER/PELTERET	KER HAND NO.	FOLIOS	DATE	LOCATION	FACSIMILE REFERENCES	CONTENTS	NOTES
804	Oxford, Bodleian Library, Ashmole 328	526	288			p. 107^6	XI^2			interlinear correction	
805	Oxford, Bodleian Library Auct. D. 2. 14, fol. 173	529.1	290		I		XI^2 or XI ex.	Bury St Edmunds	ASMMF 7	booklist	
806	Oxford, Bodleian Library Auct. D. 2. 14, fol. 173	529.1	290		2		XI^2 or XI ex.	Bury St Edmunds		additions to booklist	
807	Oxford, Bodleian Library Auct. D. 2. 14, fol. 173	529.1	290		3		XI^2 or XI ex.	Bury St Edmunds		names	*ealfric, æilwine, godric, bealde-wuine* [abbot], *freoden*
808	Oxford, Bodleian Library Auct. D. 2. 16	530	291	P 91		I*r*–2*v*	XI^2	Exeter		list of gifts	
808a	Oxford, Bodleian Library Auct. D. 2. 16	530	291	P 91		I*r*$^{10–11}$	XI^2	Exeter		interlinear addition	
809	Oxford, Bodleian Library Auct. D. 2. 16	530	291	P 91		I*v*^{2}	XI^2	Exeter		addition	
810	Oxford, Bodleian Library Auct. D. 2. 16	530	291	P 92		6*v*^{4}–7	XI^2	Exeter		Leofric ascription	
811	Oxford, Bodleian Library Auct. D. 2. 16	530	291			8*r*^{1}–14*r*^{21}	XI^2	Exeter		list of relics	
812	Oxford, Bodleian Library Auct. D. 2. 19	531	292			I*r*–55*r*^{12}, 162*r*$^{3–7}$ (the latter with some interventions by the next scribe)	X^2		ASMMF 3	gloss to gospels (Matthew, parts of Mark and John)	scribe: *farm*on, *færmen*
813	Oxford, Bodleian Library Auct. D. 2. 19	531	292			55*r*–169*r*	X^2			gloss to gospels (Luke and most of Mark and John)	scribe: *owun*
813.5	Oxford, Bodleian Library, Auct. D. 5. 3	532	293				X^1		ASMMF 7	glosses to gospels	
813.8	Oxford, Bodleian Library, Auct. F. 1. 15, fols. 1–77	533	294			ii *v*	XI	Exeter		note of ownership?	name: *brihtmærcild*
813.9	Oxford, Bodleian Library, Auct. F. 1. 15, fols. 1–77	533	294			39*v*–40*r*	XI^2	Exeter		glosses	margins

HAND NO.	LIBRARY AND SHELF-MARK	GNEUSS	KER	SAWYER/PELTERET	KER HAND NO.	FOLIOS	DATE	LOCATION	FACSIMILE REFERENCES	CONTENTS	NOTES
814	Oxford, Bodleian Library Auct. F. 1. 15, fols. 1–77	533	294			7*v*, 8*v*, 9*r*	X²	Canterbury StA		glosses to Boethius, *De consolatione philosophiae*	
◆	Oxford, Bodleian Library Auct. F. 1. 15, fols. 1–77, *see Cambridge, Corpus Christi Coll. 191*										
815	Oxford, Bodleian Library Auct. F. 1. 15, fols. 78–93	534	294	P 92		78*r*	XI²	Exeter	ASMMF 22	Leofric ascription	
816	Oxford, Bodleian Library Auct. F. 2. 14	535	295			11*r*–19*v*	XI²	Sherborne?	ASMMF 23	Lat.–OE word-list	
817	Oxford, Bodleian Library Auct. F. 2. 14	535	295			11*r*–12*v*	XI²	Sherborne?		different word-lists	
818	Oxford, Bodleian Library Auct. F. 2. 14	535	295			39*r*, 40*v*	XI ex.	Sherborne?		4 glosses to Wulfstan the Cantor, *Narratio de S. Swithuno*	
819	Oxford, Bodleian Library Auct. F. 2. 14	535	295			80*v*	XI ex.	Sherborne?		4 glosses to Phocas, *Ars grammatici*	
820	Oxford, Bodleian Library Auct. F. 3. 6	537	296			92*v*–98*v*, 124*r*–125*v*	XI¹		ASMMF 22	48 glosses to Prudentius, *Psychomachia, Peristephanon*	
821	Oxford, Bodleian Library Auct. F. 3. 6	537	296			51*r*^{14}	XI¹			1 further gloss	
822	Oxford, Bodleian Library Auct. F. 3. 6	537	296			64*r*^{4}, 98*v*^{23}	XI¹			2 more glosses	margin
823	Oxford, Bodleian Library Auct. F. 3. 6	537	296			ii *r*^{3}	XI¹			charm against a dwarf	
824	Oxford, Bodleian Library Auct. F. 3. 6	537	296			ii *v*^{16}	XI¹			note in margin	*scurfede hors* (beginning of a recipe?)
825	Oxford, Bodleian Library Auct. F. 3. 6	537	296			iii *v*$^{3-8}$	XI¹			recipe for nosebleed	
◆	Oxford, Bodleian Library Auct. F. 3. 6, *see Exeter, Cathedral 2521r*										

HAND NO.	LIBRARY AND SHELF-MARK	GNEUSS	KER	SAWYER/PELTERET	KER HAND NO.	FOLIOS	DATE	LOCATION	FACSIMILE REFERENCES	CONTENTS	NOTES
826	*unused number*										
827	Oxford, Bodleian Library Auct. F. 4. 32, fols. 1–9, 37–47	538	297			47*v*	XI²		ASMMF 16	fragmentary beginning of a penitential	
828	Oxford, Bodleian Library Auct. F. 4. 32, fols. 1–9, 37–47	538	297			47*v*	XI²			4-word addition to the last	
829	Oxford, Bodleian Library Auct. F. 4. 32, fols. 10–18	538.5	297			10*r*¹–18*v*¹⁷	XI²			homily	
830	Oxford, Bodleian Library Auct. F. 4. 32, fols. 10–18	538.5	297			10*r*–18*v*	XI/XII			alterations	
831	Oxford, Bodleian Library, Barlow 35	541	298			57*rv*	XI¹		ASMMF 15	Lat.–OE glossaries	
832	Oxford, Bodleian Library, Barlow 35	541	298			54*v*	XI¹			heading to charm for nosebleed	in lower margin
833	Oxford, Bodleian Library, Barlow 35	541	298			6*r*	XI¹			1 gloss	
834	Oxford, Bodleian Library, Barlow 35	541	298			23*r*	XI¹			1 word in margin	*wið* (probably the beginning of a charm)
834.5	Oxford, Bodleian Library, Bodley 49	542	299				X med.			10 glosses to Aldhelm, *Carmen de virginitate*	
835	Oxford, Bodleian Library, Bodley 97	545	300				XI in.	Canterbury CC?		24 glosses to Aldhelm, *De virginitate*	
836	Oxford, Bodleian Library, Bodley 97	545	300			34*r*, 46*r*, 70*v*	XI¹	Canterbury CC?		3 more glosses	
837	Oxford, Bodleian Library, Bodley 109	546	301			2*v*, 6*r*	XI¹	Canterbury StA		2 glosses to Bede, *Vita S. Cuthberti*	
838	Oxford, Bodleian Library, Bodley 130	549	302				XI ex.	Bury St Edmunds?	ASMMF 6	plant names and glosses	
839	Oxford, Bodleian Library, Bodley 155	554	303			196*v*	XI/XII	Barking		list of lands	name: *gilebeard*

HAND NO.	LIBRARY AND SHELF-MARK	GNEUSS	KER	SAWYER/PELTERET	KER HAND NO.	FOLIOS	DATE	LOCATION	FACSIMILE REFERENCES	CONTENTS	NOTES
840	Oxford, Bodleian Library, Bodley 163	555	304			152v	XI med.		ASMMF 10	Cædmon's Hymn	in margin
841	Oxford, Bodleian Library, Bodley 163	555	304			227r, 250r	XI med.			28 words in a Lat.–OE glossary, macaronic charm	
842	Oxford, Bodleian Library, Bodley 163	555	304			66r, 111v, 112r, 154r	XI in.			4 glosses to Bede, *Historia*	
842.4	Oxford, Bodleian Library, Bodley 180	555.5	305				XI/XII			OE Boethius	
842.5	Oxford, Bodleian Library, Bodley 180	555.5	305				XI/XII			corrections	
843	Oxford, Bodleian Library, Bodley 311	565	307			1r	X/XI		ASMMF 22	inscription	
844	Oxford, Bodleian Library, Bodley 311	565	307			1r	X/XI			1 gloss in penitential	
845	Oxford, Bodleian Library, Bodley 319	568	308			74r–75v	XI^1		ASMMF 22	Isidore, *De fide catholica*; continuous gloss to 1 chapter	
846	Oxford, Bodleian Library, Bodley 340 + 342	569	309				XI in.	Canterbury (or Rochester)	ASMMF 17	homilies	
847	Oxford, Bodleian Library, Bodley 340 + 342	569	309			342. 202$v$$^{8-32}$ and corrections throughout both mss	XI med.	Rochester		note on Paulinus	
848	Oxford, Bodleian Library, Bodley 340 + 342	569	309			340. 1r–52r, 98v–123r; 342. 14r–17r	XI/XII	Rochester		corrections	
849	Oxford, Bodleian Library, Bodley 340 + 342	569	309			342. 203r^{1}–206r^{14}	XI^1	Canterbury or Rochester		2 added homilies	
850	Oxford, Bodleian Library, Bodley 340 + 342	569	309			342. 206v^{1}–218r^{21}	XI^1	Rochester?		2 added homilies on St Andrew	
851	Oxford, Bodleian Library, Bodley 340 + 342	569	309			342. 203r–218r	XI/XII	Rochester?		corrections	
851.5	Oxford, Bodleian Library, Bodley 381	570	311			18v	X		ASMMF 21	1 gloss	

HAND NO.	LIBRARY AND SHELF-MARK	GNEUSS	KER	SAWYER/PELTERET	KER HAND NO.	FOLIOS	DATE	LOCATION	FACSIMILE REFERENCES	CONTENTS	NOTES
852	Oxford, Bodleian Library, Bodley 381	570	311			185*r*	X/XI	Canterbury StA?		1 gloss to John the Deacon, *Vita S. Gregorii*	
853	Oxford, Bodleian Library, Bodley 441	577	312				XI¹		ASMMF 3	gospels	
854	Oxford, Bodleian Library, Bodley 441	577	312				XI¹			corrections	
855	Oxford, Bodleian Library, Bodley 572, fols. 1–50	583	313			40*r*	X ex.	Winchester NM?		3ʳᵈ rubric to benedictional	
856	Oxford, Bodleian Library, Bodley 572, fols. 1–50	583	313			40*r*	XI¹	Winchester NM?		1ˢᵗ and 2ⁿᵈ rubrics	
857	Oxford, Bodleian Library, Bodley 572, fols. 1–50	583	313			40*r*	XI med.	Winchester NM?		cryptograms	consonant for vowel cipher
858	Oxford, Bodleian Library, Bodley 577	584	314			11*v*, 35*v*, 36*r*, 65*v*, 71*r*, 73*v*	X/XI	Canterbury CC		8 glosses to Aldhelm, *Carmen de virginitate*	
859	Oxford, Bodleian Library, Bodley 579	585	315	P 92		1*r*⁶⁻¹⁰	XI²	Exeter		Leofric ascription	
860	Oxford, Bodleian Library, Bodley 579	585	315	P 135		1*r*¹⁰⁻¹³	XI/XII	Exeter		manumission	
861	Oxford, Bodleian Library, Bodley 579	585	315	P 136–9		1*r*¹⁴–1*v*²²	XI ex.	Exeter		4 manumissions	
862	Oxford, Bodleian Library, Bodley 579	585	315	1452		11*v*¹⁸⁻¹⁹	968–93	Exeter		list of sureties	
863	Oxford, Bodleian Library, Bodley 579	585	315	1452		11*v*¹⁹⁻²³	968–93	Exeter		list of sureties (continuation)	
864	Oxford, Bodleian Library, Bodley 579	585	315	P 140		377*v*¹⁻¹⁸	XI ex.	Exeter		manumission	
865	Oxford, Bodleian Library, Bodley 579	585	315			8*v*¹⁻⁹	XI¹			manumissions	
866	Oxford, Bodleian Library, Bodley 579	585	315			8*v*¹⁰⁻¹⁴	XI¹			manumissions	

HAND NO.	LIBRARY AND SHELF-MARK	GNEUSS	KER	SAWYER/PELTERET	KER HAND NO.	FOLIOS	DATE	LOCATION	FACSIMILE REFERENCES	CONTENTS	NOTES
867	Oxford, Bodleian Library, Bodley 579	585	315			$8v^{14-16}$	XI¹			manumissions	
868	Oxford, Bodleian Library, Bodley 579	585	315			$8v^{16-18}$	XI¹			manumissions	
869	Oxford, Bodleian Library, Bodley 579	585	315			$8v^{18-20}$	XI¹			manumissions	
870	Oxford, Bodleian Library, Bodley 579	585	315			$8v^{21-3}$	XI¹			manumissions	
871	Oxford, Bodleian Library, Bodley 579	585	315			$8v^{24-7}$	XI¹			manumissions	
872	Oxford, Bodleian Library, Bodley 708	590	316	P 92		$113r$	XI²	Exeter	ASMMF 22	Leofric ascription	
873	Oxford, Bodleian Library, Bodley 865, fols. 97–112	608.1	318		1	$98v^1–98v^{22}$, $99v^{13}–102v^{22}$, $103v^{22}–107v^{15}$, $108v^{10}–110r^5$, $110r^{22}–112r^2$	XI¹			Theodulf of Orleans, *Capitula* (fragment)	precise differentiation of hands difficult
874	Oxford, Bodleian Library, Bodley 865, fols. 97–112	608.1	318		2	$103r^1–103r^{16}$	XI¹			Theodulf of Orleans, *Capitula* (fragment)	precise differentiation of hands difficult
875	Oxford, Bodleian Library, Bodley 865, fols. 97–112	608.1	318		3	$97r^{16}–98r^{22}$, $99r^1–99v^{12}$, $103r^{16}–103v^{21}$, $107v^{16}–108v^9$, $110r^6–110r^{21}$	XI¹			Theodulf of Orleans, *Capitula* (fragment)	precise differentiation of hands difficult
876	Oxford, Bodleian Library, Broxbourne 90. 28	608.5	112S				XI			Gospel fragment	
876.5	Oxford, Bodleian Library, Digby 63	611	319			$9r$	IX²	Northumbria	*ASE* 45	beginning of homily, partly in top margin, now erased	(*Men þa leofestan*) s.gað monn on ðissum bocum þæt ure ... .. (f)..e..as
876.6	Oxford, Bodleian Library, Digby 63	611	319			$25r$	X	Winchester OM ?		note in bottom margin	*xi wica*

HAND NO.	LIBRARY AND SHELF-MARK	GNEUSS	KER	SAWYER/PELTERET	KER HAND NO.	FOLIOS	DATE	LOCATION	FACSIMILE REFERENCES	CONTENTS	NOTES
876.7	Oxford, Bodleian Library, Digby 63	611	319			41r	X	Winchester OM ?		note in right margin	*for lencte(n)* against 11 March
877	Oxford, Bodleian Library, Digby 146	613	320				X ex.	Abingdon		glosses to Aldhelm, *De virginitate*, contemporary with text	
878	Oxford, Bodleian Library, Digby 146	613	320			8r–15v	XI in.	Abingdon		later glosses in small hand	
879	Oxford, Bodleian Library, Digby 146	613	320			8r–95v	XI med.	Abingdon		more than 5000 glosses	
880	Oxford, Bodleian Library, Douce 296	617					XI med.	Crowland?		names of months in a Latin calendar	
881	Oxford, Bodleian Library, Eng. bib. c. 2	621	322				XI¹		ASMMF 3	Gospel fragment	
◆	Oxford, Bodleian Library, Eng. hist. a. 2, no. I, *see Canterbury, Cathedral Library, Chart. Ant. T. 37*										
881.5	Oxford, Bodleian Library, Eng. hist. a. 2, no. II a			1546b			XI med.			bounds	
882	Oxford, Bodleian Library, Eng. hist. a. 2, no. III			405			XI¹?			bounds	
883	Oxford, Bodleian Library, Eng. hist. a. 2, no. III endorsement			1387	1v		XI med. or XI²			endorsement; bilingual, with English bounds	
883.5	Oxford, Bodleian Library, Eng. hist. a. 2, no. V			646			X med.			endorsement	
884	Oxford, Bodleian Library, Eng. hist. a. 2, no. VI			892			998	Coventry?		bounds	
885	Oxford, Bodleian Library, Eng. hist. a. 2, no. VII			916	1r¹⁸⁻²³		1007 × 1008			bounds	
886	Oxford, Bodleian Library, Eng. hist. a. 2, no. VII			916	1v		XI¹			endorsement	
887	Oxford, Bodleian Library, Eng. hist. a. 2, no. XII			1522			998			will	

HAND NO.	LIBRARY AND SHELF-MARK	GNEUSS	KER	SAWYER/PELTERET	KER HAND NO.	FOLIOS	DATE	LOCATION	FACSIMILE REFERENCES	CONTENTS	NOTES
887.1	Oxford, Bodleian Library, Eng. hist. a. 2, no. XII			1522			XI			endorsement	
◆	Oxford, Bodleian Library, Eng. hist. a. 2, no. XIII, *see London, BL, Stowe Charter 34*										
888	Oxford, Bodleian Library, Eng. hist. a. 2, no. XIV			1296			980 × 988			document in English	
889	Oxford, Bodleian Library, Eng. hist. e. 49	622	323				XI^1			Orosius	fragment
889.5	Oxford, Bodleian Library, Hatton 20	626	324		1		890 × 897		ASMMF 6 EEMF 6	Gregory (Alfred), *Regula pastoralis*	main hand
889.6	Oxford, Bodleian Library, Hatton 20	626	324		2	$6v^{12-15}$, $8r^{10-14}$, $12r^1$–$14r^5$, $15r^7$–$15v^4$, $40r^{1-13}$, $45v^{10-15}$, $46v^{6-8}$, $48v^{23}$–$49r^1$, $49r^{15}$–$53v^{19}$, $67v^{13}$–$69v^{12}$, $98v^{1-17}$				Gregory (Alfred), *Regula pastoralis*	
◆	Oxford, Bodleian Library, Hatton 20, *see London, BL, Cotton Tiberius B. xi + Kassel, Gesamthochschulbibliothek 4° Ms. theol. 131*										
◆	Oxford, Bodleian Library, Hatton 20, *see Copenhagen, Kongelige Bibliotek G. K. S. 1595*										
890	Oxford, Bodleian Library, Hatton 42	629	442 SB			49*r*	XI	Worcester?		1 gloss to *Collectio canonum Hibernensis*	
891	Oxford, Bodleian Library, Hatton 43	630	326			129*r*	XI^2	Glastonbury?		Cædmon's Hymn	
891.5	Oxford, Bodleian Library, Hatton 48	631	327			18*v*, 42*v*	IX or X		ASMMF 6	2 scribbles, top margin	*cnih, cniht ic drink*
891.6	Oxford, Bodleian Library, Hatton 48	631	327			44*v*	X/XI			name added between columns of text and in margin	*ægelmær menes*
892	Oxford, Bodleian Library, Hatton 76, fols. 1–67	632	328		1	1*r*—54*v*	XI^1	Worcester?	ASMMF 6	Gregory, *Dialogi*	

HAND NO.	LIBRARY AND SHELF-MARK	GNEUSS	KER	SAWYER/PELTERET	KER HAND NO.	FOLIOS	DATE	LOCATION	FACSIMILE REFERENCES	CONTENTS	NOTES
892a	Oxford, Bodleian Library, Hatton 76, fols. 1–67	632	328	1	55r–67v	XI[1]	Worcester?			Basil, *Admonitio*	
893	Oxford, Bodleian Library, Hatton 76, fols. 1–67	632	328	2	16v[17–18], 17r[14–27]	XI[1]	Worcester?			Gregory, *Dialogi*	
894	Oxford, Bodleian Library, Hatton 76, fols. 1–67	632	328	3	17r[1–8], 17v[12–21], 20r[7–11]	XI[1]	Worcester?			Gregory, *Dialogi*	
895	Oxford, Bodleian Library, Hatton 76, fols. 68–130a	633	328			XI med.	Worcester?			herbal	
896	Oxford, Bodleian Library, Hatton 76, fols. 68–130a	633	328		101r	XI/XII	Worcester?			copy of phrase from text	bottom margin
896.8	Oxford, Bodleian Library, Hatton 93	635	329		28r	IX[1]				leaf signature	*7 bis*
897	Oxford, Bodleian Library, Hatton 93, fol. 42	636	330		42r[5]	XI med.	Worcester?			title; rubric to single sheet of missal used as binding leaf	
898	Oxford, Bodleian Library, Hatton 113 + 114	637 638	331	1	Hatt. 113. 1r–144v; Hatt. 114. 9r–201r[6]	XI[2] (1064 × 1083)	Worcester	ASMMF 6	homilies	main hand
	Oxford, Bodleian Library, Junius 121	644	338	1	9r–137v			ASMMF 6	*Institutes of Polity*, 'Canons of Edgar', *De ecclesiasticis gradibus*, Benedictine Office, confessional and penitential texts, homilies	main hand; scribe named as *Wulfgeatus*
899	Oxford, Bodleian Library, Hatton 113 + 114	637 638	331		Hatt. 114. 1r[1]–4v[9], 201r[9]–230r[17], 236r[1]–242v[6]	XI[2]	Worcester		added quires with additional homilies	
900	Oxford, Bodleian Library, Hatton 113 + 114	637 638	331			XI[2]	Worcester		running heads	mostly Latin but occasionally in English
901	Oxford, Bodleian Library, Hatton 113 + 114	637 638	331		Hatt. 113. xi v	XI[2]	Worcester		additions to table of contents	
902	Oxford, Bodleian Library, Hatton 113 + 114	637 638	331	2	Hatt. 113. xi v; Hatt. 114. 230r[20]–235v[23], 242v[8]–246v[1]	XI[2] (after 1062)	Worcester		table of contents (some words in English), additional homilies	
	Oxford, Bodleian Library, Junius 121	644	338		120v[6] margin				correction of omission	

HAND NO.	LIBRARY AND SHELF-MARK	GNEUSS	KER	SAWYER/PELTERET	KER HAND NO.	FOLIOS	DATE	LOCATION	FACSIMILE REFERENCES	CONTENTS	NOTES
903	Oxford, Bodleian Library, Hatton 113	637	331			35r	XI^2	Worcester		addition	margin
904	Oxford, Bodleian Library, Hatton 113 + 114	637 638	331		3	Hatt. 114. 4v^{10-20}	XI^2	Worcester		added homily	
905	Oxford, Bodleian Library, Hatton 113 + 114	637 638	331		4	Hatt. 114. 5r^1–8v^{22}	XI^2	Worcester		addition to a homily	
◆	Oxford, Bodleian Library, Hatton 113 + 114, *see Cambridge, Corpus Christi Coll. 391*										
906	Oxford, Bodleian Library, Hatton 113 + 114	637 638	331		6	Hatt. 114. 247r^1–247v^7	XI^2	Worcester		added homilies	
907	Oxford, Bodleian Library, Hatton 113 + 114	637 638	331			Hatt. 113. 67v^{18}, 109r^{20}, and perhaps 72r^{22}	XI^2	Worcester		alterations to text	
908	Oxford, Bodleian Library, Hatton 113 + 114	637 638	331			Hatt. 114. 3$v^{3,\,5}$, 17r^1, 18$v^{9,\,12}$, 19$r^{10,\,11}$, 26r^5, 28v^1, 29v^{22}, 31r^4, 37r^6, 39r^{15}, 39v^{21}, 40r^1, 44r^{22}, 45r^8, 46r^2, 74r^7, 75$v^{17,\,18,\,21}$, 84v^{18}, 94v^7, 95v^{10}, 96v^{23}, 97$v^{10,\,12}$, 97*r^4, 97*v^{12}, 99v^5, 100r^{12}, 100v^{18}, 105v^{23}, 123r^{16-18}, 132r^5, 147v^4, 150$v^{1,\,2,\,12}$, 151r^9, 155r^9, 164r^3, 166v^{21}, 167r^4, 180$r^{16,\,18,\,\text{foot}}$, 190$r^{23}$, 198$v^8$, 229$v^2$, 240$v^{14}$, 242$r^{10,\,13}$	XI^2	Worcester		alterations in brown ink, often linked to text by long descenders	
	Oxford, Bodleian Library, Junius 121	644	338			24v^3, (24v^{18}?), 39$v^{10,\,11}$, 121v^{16}, 149v^{14-23}, 150r^3, 151v^{10}, 152r^8					
909	Oxford, Bodleian Library, Hatton 113 + 114	637 638	331			Hatt. 114. 19$r^{\text{bottom margin}}$	XI^2	Worcester		note on free will	

HAND NO.	LIBRARY AND SHELF-MARK	GNEUSS	KER	SAWYER/PELTERET	KER HAND NO.	FOLIOS	DATE	LOCATION	FACSIMILE REFERENCES	CONTENTS	NOTES
910	Oxford, Bodleian Library, Hatton 113 + 114	637 638	331			Hatt. 114. 26v^{19}, 27v^{21}, 28r^{20}, 42r^{24}, 42v^{1}	XI²	Worcester		additions to text in brown ink	
911	Oxford, Bodleian Library, Hatton 113 + 114	637 638	331			Hatt. 114. 20v^{5-6}, 29v^{6}, 37r^{16}, 40v^{21}, 41r^{5}, 42$r^{4, 14}$, 43r^{4}, 55r^{1}, 62v^{20}, 63v^{12}, 72r^{21}, 91$r^{21, 23}$, 97*r^{17}, 118v^{4}, 146v^{3}, 190$r^{12, 16, 21}$, 191r^{2}, 191v^{1}, 193r^{3}, 196r^{4}, 197r^{1}, 197v^{6-7}, 215v^{7}, 223r^{23}, 237r^{18}, 243$r^{4-6, 8, 11, 20, 23}$	XI²	Worcester		additions in dark ink and slightly scratchy nib, often insterted with colon	
912	Oxford, Bodleian Library, Hatton 113 + 114	637 638	331			Hatt. 114. 36v^{13}	XI²	Worcester		alternative opening	
913	Oxford, Bodleian Library, Hatton 113 + 114	637 638	331			Hatt. 114. 42r bottom margin	XI²	Worcester		doxology as alternative ending	distinctive fine hand
914	Oxford, Bodleian Library, Hatton 113 + 114	637 638	331			Hatt. 114. 49$v^{5, 13, 20-2}$, 50r^{13}, 50v^{16}, 52r^{14}, 53v^{14}, 55$v^{5, 10, 14, 21}$, 56r^{6}, 56v^{7}	XI²	Worcester		frequent alterations to a successive group of homilies in a fine pen	
915	Oxford, Bodleian Library, Hatton 113 + 114	637 638	331			Hatt. 114. 181r^{5}	XI²	Worcester		expanded ending in brown ink	
916	Oxford, Bodleian Library, Hatton 113 + 114	637 638	331			Hatt. 113. 107r^{10}; Hatt. 114. 71r^{12}, 81$r^{3, 7}$, 81v^{6}, 90v^{21}, 94$r^{6, 16}$, 95$r^{1, 3}$, 95v^{5}, 96r^{2}, 96$v^{20, 23}$, 97$r^{1, 6}$, 97$v^{3, 11, 17}$, 123r^{1}, 123v^{14}, 152v^{11}	XI²	Worcester		variant readings introduced by *uel* probably in at least two hands	
	Oxford, Bodleian Library, Junius 121	644	338			147r^{20}					
917	Oxford, Bodleian Library, Hatton 113 + 114	637 638	331			Hatt. 114. 132$r^{5, 7, 9}$	XI²	Worcester		correction of omission and minor changes	

HAND NO.	LIBRARY AND SHELF-MARK	GNEUSS	KER	SAWYER/PELTERET	KER HAND NO.	FOLIOS	DATE	LOCATION	FACSIMILE REFERENCES	CONTENTS	NOTES
918	Oxford, Bodleian Library, Hatton 113 + 114	637 638	331			Hatt. 114. 200v, 201r	XI²	Worcester		running heads	
919	Oxford, Bodleian Library, Hatton 113 + 114	637 638	331			Hatt. 113. 5r^1, 5v^{12}, 6v^3, 7r^8, 7r^9, 19r^{16}, 21r^4, 40v^{20}, 58r^{17}, 71r^{20}, 71v^1, 76r^{20}, 77v^{10}, 78r^{16}, 119r^{19}; Hatt. 114. 42v^1, 53r^7, 70r^{13}, 72v^{19}, 73r^{11}, 73v^3, 76r^6, 86r^4, 96r^4, 97*v^6, 98r^{19}, 105$v^{10,\,11}$, 109r^1, 116v^{13}, 119r^4, 123v^7, 131r^{17}, 132r^{20}, 138v^{12}, 140v^{14}, 155v^1, 160v^{23}, 176v^{19-21}, 177r^{12}, 246r^3	XI²	Worcester		minor additions in margins and interlinear in more than one hand	
♦	Oxford, Bodleian Library, Hatton 113 + 114, *see Cambridge, Corpus Christi Coll. 178, Part A*										
920	Oxford, Bodleian Library, Hatton 115 + Lawrence, Univ. of Kansas, Kenneth Spencer Research Lib., Pryce C2. 2	639	332S			Hatt. 115. 1–64, 66–7; Pryce 68–139	XI²		ASMMF 6 ASMMF 7	homilies	
921	Oxford, Bodleian Library, Hatton 115 + Lawrence, Univ. of Kansas, Kenneth Spencer Research Lib., Pryce C2. 2	639	332S			Hatt. 115. 140r^1–147r^9	XI med.			additional booklet containing one homily	
922	Oxford, Bodleian Library, Hatton 115 + Lawrence, Univ. of Kansas, Kenneth Spencer Research Lib., Pryce C2. 2	639	332S			143v^3–146r	XI²			corrections to the added homily	
923	Oxford, Bodleian Library, Hatton 115 + Lawrence, Univ. of Kansas, Kenneth Spencer Research Lib., Pryce C2. 2	639	332S			Hatt. 115. 65r^2–65v^{14}	XI ex.			exhortation	added leaf

HAND NO.	LIBRARY AND SHELF-MARK	GNEUSS	KER	SAWYER/PELTERET	KER HAND NO. FOLIOS	DATE	LOCATION	FACSIMILE REFERENCES	CONTENTS	NOTES
924	Oxford, Bodleian Library, Hatton 115 + Lawrence, Univ. of Kansas, Kenneth Spencer Research Lib., Pryce C2. 2	639	332S		Hatt. 115. 65v^{17-21}	XI ex.			'Wulfstan' exhortation	
925	Oxford, Bodleian Library, Junius 11	640	334		pp. 1–212	X/XI	Canterbury CC?	Gollancz, 1927	scriptural poems	
926	Oxford, Bodleian Library, Junius 11	640	334		pp. 213–15	XI¹	Canterbury CC?		*'Christ and Satan'* (part)	
926a	Oxford, Bodleian Library, Junius 11	640	334		pp. 213–15	XI¹	Canterbury CC?		alterations	
927	Oxford, Bodleian Library, Junius 11	640	334		pp. 216–28	XI¹	Canterbury CC?		*'Christ and Satan'* (part)	
928	Oxford, Bodleian Library, Junius 11	640	334		p. 229	XI¹	Canterbury CC?		*'Christ and Satan'* (end)	
929	Oxford, Bodleian Library, Junius 11	640	334		p. 2	XI¹	Canterbury CC?		name on image	*ælfwine*
929.5	Oxford, Bodleian Library, Junius 11	640	334		p. 211	XI¹	Canterbury CC?		1 word in margin	innan
929.7	Oxford, Bodleian Library, Junius 27	641	335			X¹	Winchester?		continuous interlinear psalter gloss	
930	Oxford, Bodleian Library, Junius 85 + 86	642	336		2r, 17r–17v, 35r^5–81r	XI med.	Kent	ASMMF 17	homilies, titles to charms	the precise point of the shifts between 930 and 930a is disputed, if indeed there are two hands
930a	Oxford, Bodleian Library, Junius 85 + 86	642	336		2v, 12r–16v, 25r–35r^4	XI med.	Kent		*Visio Pauli*, homilies	
930b	Oxford, Bodleian Library, Junius 85 + 86	642	336		18r–24r^{12}	XI med.	Kent		homily	added quire, cut down for insertion, with words added by hand 930

HAND NO.	LIBRARY AND SHELF-MARK	GNEUSS	KER	SAWYER/PELTERET	KER HAND NO.	FOLIOS	DATE	LOCATION	FACSIMILE REFERENCES	CONTENTS	NOTES
◆	Oxford, Bodleian Library, Junius 121, *see Oxford, Bodleian Lib., Hatton 113 + 114*										
◆	Oxford, Bodleian Library, Junius 121, *see Cambridge, Corpus Christi Coll. 391*										
931	Oxford, Bodleian Library, Junius 121	644	338		6	$138r^{1}$–$148v^{9}$	XI²	Worcester	ASMMF 6	two homilies, the first of a number added to the original manuscript	
932	Oxford, Bodleian Library, Junius 121	644	338		7	$149r^{1-23}$, $150v^{1-15}$, $151v^{1-22}$	XI²	Worcester		parts of a homily	
933	Oxford, Bodleian Library, Junius 121	644	338		8	$154r^{1-16}$	XI²	Worcester		other parts of the same homily	
934	Oxford, Bodleian Library, Junius 121	644	338		9	$154v^{13}$–$157r^{3}$	XI²	Worcester		one homily	
935	Oxford, Bodleian Library, Junius 121	644	338		10	$157r^{6}$–$160r^{15}$	XI ex.	Worcester		one homily	
936	Oxford, Bodleian Library, Junius 121	644	338			$27r$, $28r^{8}$, $76v^{2-3}$, $81v^{10}$, $95v^{15}$, $104r^{10}$, $129r^{17}$, $141v^{16}$, $148r^{5, 7}$, $148v^{13}$, $149r^{15}$	XI²	Worcester		alterations in more than one hand	
937	Oxford, Bodleian Library, Junius 121	644	338			$1r$	XI ex.	Worcester		pen trial	*writ ðus*
938	Oxford, Bodleian Library, Lat. th. c. 4	652	340			$1r$	XI in.	Worcester ?		1 gloss to Sedulius, *Carmen paschale*	
939	Oxford, Bodleian Library, Laud Misc. 482	656	343				XI med. or XI²	Worcester	ASMMF 6	penitential and confessional texts	main hand
940	Oxford, Bodleian Library, Laud Misc. 482	656	343			$7r^{1}$–$8r^{8}$, $8v^{8-24}$	XI med. or XI²	Worcester		penitential and confessional texts	
941	Oxford, Bodleian Library, Laud Misc. 509 + London, BL, Cotton Vespasian D. xxi, fols. 18–40	657	344		1	Laud $1r$–$15r^{7}$, $15r^{22-9}$, $15v^{11}$–$17r^{11}$, $17r^{23}$–$141v$; Vesp. $18r$–$40v$	XI²		ASMMF 7	pentateuch, Ælfric, Letter to Wulfgeat, On the Old and New Testament, OE *Life of St Guthlac*	

HAND NO.	LIBRARY AND SHELF-MARK	GNEUSS	KER	SAWYER/PELTERET	KER HAND NO.	FOLIOS	DATE	LOCATION	FACSIMILE REFERENCES	CONTENTS	NOTES
942	Oxford, Bodleian Library, Laud Misc. 509 + London, BL, Cotton Vespasian D. xxi, fols. 18–40	657	344		2	Laud 15r^{8-21}, 15v^{1-10}	XI^2			pentateuch	
943	Oxford, Bodleian Library, Laud Misc. 509 + London, BL, Cotton Vespasian D. xxi, fols. 18–40	657	344		3	Laud 17r^{11-23}	XI^2			pentateuch	
943a	Oxford, Bodleian Library, Laud Misc. 509 + London, BL, Cotton Vespasian D. xxi, fols. 18–40	657	344			Laud 66v^6	XI^2			1 gloss to Latin gloss on Leviticus	
943b	Oxford, Bodleian Library, Laud Misc. 509 + London, BL, Cotton Vespasian D. xxi, fols. 18–40	657	344			Laud 112r^8	XI^2			1 variant reading	
944	Oxford, Bodleian Library, Rawlinson C. 697	661	349			1r–16r	X med./X^2	Glastonbury?	ASMMF 23	glosses to Aldhelm, *Ænigmata*	
945	Oxford, Bodleian Library, Rawlinson C. 697	661	349			17r–64r	X med./X^2	Glastonbury?		glosses to Aldhelm, *Carmen de virginitate*	
946	Oxford, Bodleian Library, Rawlinson G. 57 + G. III	664	350			G.57. 1r–5v	XI ex. or XI/XII			113 glosses to *Disticha Catonis*	Parchment is dark and writing is tiny; differentiation of hands difficult
947	Oxford, Bodleian Library, Rawlinson G. 57 + G. III	664	350			G.57. 6r–27r	XI ex. or XI/XII			8 glosses to *Ilias Latina*	
948	Oxford, Bodleian Library, Rawlinson G. 57 + G. III	664	350			G.III. 1r–16r	XI ex. or XI/XII			33 glosses to Avianus, *Fabulae*	
948.2	Oxford, Bodleian Library, Tanner 10	668	351		1		X^1		EEMF 24	Bede, *Ecclesiastical History*	main hand
948.3	Oxford, Bodleian Library, Tanner 10	668	351		2	103r^1–104r^5, 115v^1–117v^{13}	X^1			Bede, *Ecclesiastical History*	occasional interventions by main hand in hand 2 second stint
948.4	Oxford, Bodleian Library, Tanner 10	668	351		3	105r–115r^{21}	X med.			Bede, *Ecclesiastical History*	115r erased and rewritten
948.5	Oxford, Bodleian Library, Tanner 10	668	351		4	117v^{13}–126r^{23}, 132r^1–139v^{23}	X^1			Bede, *Ecclesiastical History*	

HAND NO.	LIBRARY AND SHELF-MARK	GNEUSS	KER	SAWYER/PELTERET	KER HAND NO.	FOLIOS	DATE	LOCATION	FACSIMILE REFERENCES	CONTENTS	NOTES
948.6	Oxford, Bodleian Library, Tanner 10	668	351		5	$126v^1$–$131v^{23}$	X^1			Bede, *Ecclesiastical History*	
948.7	Oxford, Bodleian Library, Tanner 10	668	351			$83r$				name in margin	*Godmær*
949	Oxford, Brasenose College, Latham M. 6. 15	670	352				XI^1		ASMMF 16	homily fragment	
950	Oxford, Corpus Christi College 197	672	353			$1r$–105	X^2	Worcester?		Benedictine Rule in Latin and English	
951	Oxford, Corpus Christi College 197	672	353				XI			titles to chaps. 2, 7	
952	Oxford, Corpus Christi College 197	672	353				XI			corrections throughout the text	
953	Oxford, Corpus Christi College 197	672	353			$106v^1$–$108r^6$	XI med.	Bury St Edmunds		list of possessions and rents	added quires containing Bury documents
954	Oxford, Corpus Christi College 197	672	353			$108r^{7-11}$	XI^2	Bury St Edmunds		land grant	
955	Oxford, Corpus Christi College 197	672	353			$108r^{11-12}$	XI^2	Bury St Edmunds		end of notice of grant	
956	Oxford, Corpus Christi College 197	672	353			$108r^{14-21}$	XI^2	Bury St Edmunds		notices of land grants	
957	Oxford, Corpus Christi College 197	672	353			$108r^{21-3}$	XI ex.	Bury St Edmunds		added notice	
958	Oxford, Corpus Christi College 197	672	353			$108r^{1-6}$	XI/XII	Bury St Edmunds		glosses to roman numerals	
959	Oxford, Corpus Christi College 279, Pt II	673	354		1		XI in.			OE Bede	main hand
960	Oxford, Corpus Christi College 279, Pt II	673	354		2	$11v^{10-20}$, $22v^{1-3}$, $22v^{16-26}$, $69v^1$–$70r^{10}$, $83v^7$–$84r^9$, $101v^{10}$–$102v^{24}$, $106r^{10}$–$109r^{24}$, $111r^1$–$113r^{24}$, $117v^{14-24}$, $120r^4$–$121v^{24}$, $124v^1$–$125r^{24}$, $129r^{1-14}$, $138v^{17}$–$140v^{23}$, $147v^{1-12}$, $148r^{14-23}$, $148v^9$–$149v^8$	XI in.			OE Bede	

HAND NO.	LIBRARY AND SHELF-MARK	GNEUSS	KER	SAWYER/PELTERET	KER HAND NO.	FOLIOS	DATE	LOCATION	FACSIMILE REFERENCES	CONTENTS	NOTES
961	Oxford, Corpus Christi College 279, Pt II	673	354		3	$47r^{1-26}$	XI in.			OE Bede	
962	Oxford, Corpus Christi College 279, Pt II	673	354			mainly 87–108, 149–52	XI^1			corrections	
963	Oxford, Corpus Christi College 279, Pt II	673	354				XI^1			further corrections	
964	Oxford, Oriel College 3	680	358				XI in.	Canterbury CC		5 glosses to Prudentius anthology	
965	Oxford, Oriel College 34, fols. 57–153	681	359				XI^1			1 gloss to Bede, *In epistolas catholicas*	
966	Oxford, St John's College 28	684	361				X/XI	Canterbury StA?		2 glosses to Gregory, *Regula pastoralis*	
967	Oxford, St John's College 154	686	362			$1r^1$–$116v^4$	XI in.		ASMMF 15	Ælfric, *Grammar*	
968	Oxford, St John's College 154	686	362			$116v^4$–$160r^{21}$ and glosses to $160v$–$221v^{14}$	XI in.			Ælfric, *Grammar* and *Glossary*	
969	Oxford, St John's College 154	686	362				XI ex.			marginalia to the grammar	
970	Oxford, St John's College 154	686	362			$160v$–$221v$	XI^2			very many glosses to Ælfric Bata's Colloquies, to an anonymous colloquy, and to lists of hard words abstracted from Ælfric's *Grammar*	
971	Oxford, St John's College 154	686	362			e.g. $192v$	XI^2			added glosses in a smaller hand	
972	Oxford, St John's College 154	686	362			$198r^7$	XI^2			gloss	*cycene*
973	Oxford, St John's College 154	686	362			$198r^{10,\,14,\,18}$, $198v^7$, etc.	XI^2			added glosses in several later hands	
974	Oxford, St John's College 154	686	362			$221v^{15}$–$222r^{21}$	XI ex.			continuous gloss to Abbo of St Germain, *Bella Parisiacae urbis*	
975	Paris, Archives nationales K 19, no. 6A			1105		$1r^{1-5}$	1053 × 1057			writ	
976	Paris, Archives nationales K 19, no. 6B			1028		$1r^{16-25}$	1059 or XI/XII			bounds	

HAND NO.	LIBRARY AND SHELF-MARK	GNEUSS	KER	SAWYER/PELTERET	KER HAND NO.	FOLIOS	DATE	LOCATION	FACSIMILE REFERENCES	CONTENTS	NOTES
977	*unused number*										
978	Paris, Bibliothèque Nationale, anglais 67	876	363				XI¹		ASMMF 15	Ælfric, *Grammar*	fragment
979	Paris, Bibliothèque Nationale, lat. 943	879	364			156r–160r	X/XI	Sherborne	ASMMF 22	homily	
980	Paris, Bibliothèque Nationale, lat. 943	879	364			163v¹⁻¹⁴	XI in.	Sherborne		rules of confraternity (part)	
981	Paris, Bibliothèque Nationale, lat. 943	879	364			163v¹⁴⁻³²	XI in.	Sherborne		conclusion of the rules	
982	Paris, Bibliothèque Nationale, lat. 943	879	364			164r–170r¹	XI in.	Sherborne		homily	
983	Paris, Bibliothèque Nationale, lat. 943	879	364	1383		170v	XI¹	Sherborne		writ	*æþelric* (b. of Sherborne), *æþelmær*
984	Paris, Bibliothèque Nationale, lat. 2825, fols. 57–81	882	365			58v, 59r, 65v, 68r, 71r, 75r	X/XI			7 glosses to Bede, *Vita S. Cuthberti*	
985	Paris, Bibliothèque Nationale, lat. 7585	889	366			139r	XI¹			1 gloss to Isidore, *Etymologiae*	
986	Paris, Bibliothèque Nationale, lat. 7585	889	366			238v	XI¹			Ælfric, *De falsis diis* (part)	
987	Paris, Bibliothèque Nationale, lat. 8092	890	425B				XI med.			46 glosses to Sedulius, *Carmen paschale*	
988	Paris, Bibliothèque Nationale, lat. 8824	891	367			1r–175v	XI med.		EEMF 8	bilingual psalter	scribe: wulfwine 'cada'
989	Paris, Bibliothèque Nationale, lat. 10575	896	370			163r	X²			form of absolution	added slip
990	Paris, Bibliothèque Nationale, lat. 10575	896	370			178v¹⁻¹⁰	X²			farming memoranda: list of livestock and farm workers	mostly erased
991	Paris, Bibliothèque Nationale, lat. 10575	896	370	1602		178v	X²			bounds	erased but visible with reagent
992	Paris, Bibliothèque Nationale, nouv. acq. lat. 586, fols. 16–131	902	371				XI¹			18 glosses to '*Excerptiones de Prisciano*'	

HAND NO.	LIBRARY AND SHELF-MARK	GNEUSS	KER	SAWYER/PELTERET	KER HAND NO.	FOLIOS	DATE	LOCATION	FACSIMILE REFERENCES	CONTENTS	NOTES
992.5	Paris, Bibliothèque Sainte-Geneviève 2410	903	G4			120v	XI[1]	Canterbury		1 gloss to Ovid, *Amores*	
◆	Philadelphia Free Library, John Frederick Lewis Collection ET 121, *see Cambridge, University Library Add. 3330*										
993	Princeton, University Library, The Scheide Library, 71	905	382S		1		X/XI		EEMF 10, ASMMF 17	homilies	main hand
994	Princeton, University Library, The Scheide Library, 71	905	382S		2	50r2–3, 65r5–21, 67r7–68v6, 84r1–84v6, 86r1–21, 86v2–21, 103v16–104r21, 109r6–15, 110v13–15, 120r1–139v21	X/XI			homilies	
995	Princeton, University Library, The Scheide Library, 71	905	382S			72r8 and top margin	XI ex. or XI/XII			added explanatory note	
996	Princeton, University Library, The Scheide Library, 71	905	382S			70v2, 98v10	XI[2]			added titles	
997	Princeton, University Library, The Scheide Library, 71	905	382S			104r18	XI[2]			additional titles	
998	Princeton, University Library, The Scheide Library, 71	905	382S			14r10–16r16	XI			alterations	inserted *se* before *hælend*
999	Princeton, University Library, The Scheide Library, 71	905	382S				XI			occasional corrections throughout	
1000	Princeton, University Library, The Scheide Library, M. 140			1497			X[2]		Whitelock, 1968	will	
1001	Ripon, Cathedral Library, MS frag. 2	696	372				XI		ASMMF 14	1 gloss to hymnal	
◆	Rome, *see Vatican City*										
1002	Rouen, Bibliothèque Municipale 274 (Y. 6)	921	377			207r–212v, 6r–11v	XI[1]	Peterborough or Ely	ASMMF 18	missal rubrics, names of months	
1003	Rouen, Bibliothèque Municipale 368 (A. 27)	922	374			172v	XI[1]			gloss to benedictional	

HAND NO.	LIBRARY AND SHELF-MARK	GNEUSS	KER	SAWYER/PELTERET	KER HAND NO.	FOLIOS	DATE	LOCATION	FACSIMILE REFERENCES	CONTENTS	NOTES
1004	*unused number*										
1005	Rouen, Bibliothèque Municipale 368 (A. 27)	922	374			Ir	XI¹		ASMMF 18	pen trial	bottom margin: *wryt ðus oððe bæt*
1005.1	Rouen, Bibliothèque Municipale 368 (A. 27)	922	374			195v²	XI¹			pen trial	*ðis wrat ... on þise bæc* or *bæc* (omission is erasure, presumably of a name)
1005.2	Rouen, Bibliothèque Municipale 368 (A. 27)	922	374			196r	XI¹			note of ownership	*Lyuinc b* [bishop of Crediton, or bishop of Wells and subsequently archbishop of Canterbury] *ah þas boc*
1006	Rouen, Bibliothèque Municipale 1385 (U. 107), fols. 28–85	927	376			80v	XI¹	Winchester OM	ASMMF 18	3 Latin words added in margin and glossed	
1006.1	St Gallen, Stiftsbibliothek, cod. 254		App. 25			p. 254a⁶⁻¹¹	X²		ASMMF 26	Bede's Death Song, written by a continental hand using a Northumbrian copy	
1006.2	St-Omer, Bibliothèque d'Aglomération de St-Omer 150		App. 30			76ra¹¹, 76ra²²	X		ASMMF 18	two glosses	
1006.4	St Petersburg, Russian National Library, O. v. XVI. 1, fols. 1–16	844	415			15r	X		ASMMF 26	maxim	
1006.5	St Petersburg, Russian National Library, O. v. XVI. 1, fols. 1–16	844	415			15r	X			incomplete text of the same maxim	
1006.7	St Petersburg, Russian National Library, Q. v. I. 18	846	122			107r	VIII (731 × 746)	Wearmouth-Jarrow	ASMMF 26	Caedmon's Hymn in lower margin	
1007	Salisbury, Cathedral Library 38	707	378				X ex.	Canterbury		many glosses to Aldhelm, *De virginitate*	not clear how many hands
1008	Salisbury, Cathedral Library 38	707	378				X ex.	Canterbury		further glosses in at least one more hand (hands are tiny and difficult to distinguish)	
1009	Salisbury, Cathedral Library 38	707	378				XI¹	Canterbury		larger hand	

HAND NO.	LIBRARY AND SHELF-MARK	GNEUSS	KER	SAWYER/PELTERET	KER HAND NO.	FOLIOS	DATE	LOCATION	FACSIMILE REFERENCES	CONTENTS	NOTES
1010	Salisbury, Cathedral Library 150, fols. 1–151	740	379			12r–149v	XI/XII	Shaftesbury?		continuous gloss to psalter and canticles	
1011	Salisbury, Cathedral Library 150, fols. 1–151	740	379			149v–151v	X²	Shaftesbury?		gloss to Athanasian Creed	
1012	Salisbury, Cathedral Library 172	751	380			50v	X²	Canterbury?		1 gloss to Augustine, *Enchiridion*	
1013	Salisbury, Cathedral Library 173	752	381			92v	XI¹	Salisbury?		3 word scribble (copyist's note?)	*her ic let*
1014	Salisbury, Cathedral Library 173	752	381			141v	XI¹	Salisbury?		name	*æþelmær*
1015	Salisbury, Cathedral Library 173	752	381			142v	XI¹	Salisbury?		5 word scribble	*þem þe beo þas word*
1015.3	Salzburg, Carolino-Augusteum Musaeum, 2163	App. 32				12r	IX			OE words in Latin sentences copied by a continental scribe	
1015.5	Sens, Musées de Sens (Trésor de la Cathedral)		383				IX¹?		ASMMF 26	label from relic	12 words on verso
◆	Sigmaringen, *see now Bloomington, Indiana University, Lilly Library, Add. 1000*										
◆	Sonderhausen, Schlossmuseum, Lat. liturg. XI. 1, *see Cambridge, Pembroke College 312, C nos 1, 2*										
◆	Spangenberg, Pfarrbibliothek, *see now Marburg, Hessisches Staatarchiv*										
1016	Stafford, William Salt Library 84/1/41			602		1r¹¹⁻¹⁴	XI²			bounds	
1017	Stafford, William Salt Library 84/1/41			602		1v	XI²			note of ownership	
1018	Stafford, William Salt Library 84/1/41			602		1v	XI²			further note	
1019	Stafford, William Salt Library 84/2/41			768			968 or XI			bounds	

HAND NO.	LIBRARY AND SHELF-MARK	GNEUSS	KER	SAWYER/PELTERET	KER HAND NO.	FOLIOS	DATE	LOCATION	FACSIMILE REFERENCES	CONTENTS	NOTES
1019.5	Stafford, William Salt Library 84/3/41			879			XI²			bounds (forgery)	
1020	Stafford, William Salt Library 84/4/41			878	1r¹⁻³⁰		996	Kent?		bounds	
1021	Stafford, William Salt Library 84/5/41			922	1r⁷⁻⁸		1009			bounds	
◆	Stafford, William Salt Library S. 7, *see Exeter, Cathedral 2517*										
1021.5	Stockholm, Kungliga biblioteket, A 135	937	385	1204a	11r		IX med.	Canterbury CC	EEMF 28–29 Codex aureus ASMMF 26	inscription in upper and lower margins	names: *ælfred* (ealdorman), *werburg* (his wife)
1022	Taunton, Somerset County Record Office DD / CC 111489			553	1r¹²⁻²³		XI/XII			bounds	
1023	Taunton, Somerset County Record Office DD / CC 111489			553	1v		XI/XII			endorsement	
1024	Taunton, Somerset County Record Office DD / SAS C / 1193 / 77		G7				XI med./ XI²			homiletic fragments in Latin and English	fragment
1024.7	Vatican City, Biblioteca Apostolica Vaticana, Pal. lat. 68, fols. 1–46	909	388		12v, 15r, 20v		VIII		ASMMF 27	scholia	5 glosses
1025	Vatican City, Biblioteca Apostolica Vaticana, Reg. lat. 204	913	389				XI¹	Canterbury StA	ASMMF 27	16 glosses to Bede, Life of St Cuthbert	
1026	Vatican City, Biblioteca Apostolica Vaticana, Reg. lat. 338, fols. 64–123	914	390S		91r¹⁸⁻²²		XI¹		ASMMF 27	charm	
1027	Vatican City, Biblioteca Apostolica Vaticana, Reg. lat. 338, fols. 64–123	914	390S		111r		XI¹			heading of a charm	
1028	Vatican City, Biblioteca Apostolica Vaticana, Reg. lat. 497, fol. 71	916	391				XI¹		ASMMF 27	Orosius fragment	
1029	Vatican City, Biblioteca Apostolica Vaticana, Reg. lat. 946, fols. 72–6	917	392		75v		XI¹		ASMMF 27	law fragment	
1030	Vatican City, Biblioteca Apostolica Vaticana, Reg. lat. 946, fols. 72–6	917	392		75v		XI¹			marginal addition supplying lost text	

HAND NO.	LIBRARY AND SHELF-MARK	GNEUSS	KER	SAWYER/PELTERET	KER HAND NO.	FOLIOS	DATE	LOCATION	FACSIMILE REFERENCES	CONTENTS	NOTES
1031	Vatican City, Biblioteca Apostolica Vaticana, Reg. lat. 1283, fol. 114	918	393			114v	XI^1		ASMMF 27	Ælfric, *De temporibus anni*	fragment
1032	Vercelli, Biblioteca Capitolare CXVII	941	394				X^2	Canterbury?	EEMF 19	homilies and saints' lives in prose and verse	main hand
1033	Vercelli, Biblioteca Capitolare CXVII	941	394			$41v^{24}$	X^2	Canterbury?		name	*eadgiþ*
1034	Vercelli, Biblioteca Capitolare CXVII	941	394			$63v^{foot}$	XI^1	Canterbury?		pen trial	*writ þus*
1035	Vercelli, Biblioteca Capitolare CXVII	941	394			$99r^{8}$	XI^2?	Canterbury?		interlinear insertions	*his, sclean*
1036	Washington, D. C., Folger Shakespeare Library, printed book binding	943.2	426B				XI			strip of parchment with unknown text	
1037	Wells, Cathedral Library 7	758	395				XI med.			bilingual Benedictine Rule	fragment
1038	Wells, Cathedral Library 7	758	395				XI med.			some chapter titles	
1038.5	Wells, DC, Cathedral Charter 1			677			X med. (958)			bounds and endorsement	
	Westminster, *see London*										
1038.8	Winchester, Cathedral Library, Showcase			649			X med.			bounds and endorsement	
1039	Winchester, Cathedral Library 1 + London, BL, Cotton Tiberius D. iv, vol. 2, fols. 158–66	759	396			81r	XI med.			Cædmon's Hymn in margin	
1040	Winchester, Winchester College, Muniment Room, WCM 12090			360			XI^1			bounds	
1040.5	Winchester, Winchester College, Muniment Room, WCM 12091			470			X med.			bounds and endorsement	
1041	Winchester, Winchester College, Muniment Room, WCM 12093			956		$1r^{16-18}$	1019			bounds	
1041.5	Worcester, Cathedral Library, Add. mss			59			VIII^2			bounds	

HAND NO.	LIBRARY AND SHELF-MARK	GNEUSS	KER	SAWYER/PELTERET	KER HAND NO.	FOLIOS	DATE	LOCATION	FACSIMILE REFERENCES	CONTENTS	NOTES
1042	Worcester, Cathedral Library F. 173	764	397			24r	XI med.	Winchester OM		heading to an order of burial	
1043	Worcester, Cathedral Library Q. 5	765	399				X ex.	Canterbury CC		2 glosses to Bede, *De arte metrica*	
1044	Worcester, Cathedral Library Q. 5	765	399			78v	XI med.			charm	
1044.5	Würzburg, Universitätsbibliothek, M. p. th. q. 2	944	401			Ir	VIII			4-word inscription	name: *cuthsuuithae* (abbess)
1044.6	Würzburg, Universitätsbibliothek, M. p. th. q. 2	944	401			Ir	VIII			repeated word of inscription	*abbatissan*
1045	York, Minster Library, Add. 1, fols. 10–161	774	402S			156v^{1-12}, 158r^1–159v^{24}	XI¹	York	Barker, 1968; ASMMF 14	list of property; homilies	
1046	York, Minster Library, Add. 1, fols. 10–161	774	402S			156v^{13-18}	XI¹	York		two further lists	
1047	York, Minster Library, Add. 1, fols. 10–161	774	402S			157r^{1-7}	XI¹	York		list of property	
1048	York, Minster Library, Add. 1, fols. 10–161	774	402S			157r^{10-28}	XI¹	York		lists of property	
◆	York, Minster Library, Add. 1, fols. 10–161, *see Copenhagen, Kongelige Bibliotek G. K. S. 1595*										
1049	York, Minster Library, Add. 1, fols. 10–161	774	402S			160r^1–160v^{26}	XI¹	York		writ	
1050	York, Minster Library, Add. 1, fols. 10–161	774	402S			161r^{1-5}	XI med.	York		inventory	
1051	York, Minster Library, Add. 1, fols. 10–161	774	402S			161v^{1-17}	XI¹	York		bidding prayers	
1052	York, Minster Library, Add. 1, fols. 10–161	774	402S			161v^{18-29}	XI²	York		list of names	

Index of Names

This list includes names found in the margins of manuscripts and within short texts, all noted in the *Conspectus* above. It excludes names in documents and lists of names in a Liber Vitae. Writers identifying themselves (or others) as scribes appear here in bold, while those who are assumed to have written texts or marginalia (e.g. Ælfric of Eynsham) are in italic.

Æadgares: *see* Eadgar
Ædwi 189
Ægelmær menes 891.6
Ælfgyþ 332
Ælfmær 14
Ælfmær Pattafox 628.1
Ælfnoð Ælrices sunu 275
Ælfred (ealdorman) 1021.5
Ælfric 367
Ælfric Cild 628.1
Ælfric Wulfrices (sunu) 637
Ælfric of Bath 52
Ælfric of Eynsham 712
Ælfstan 724
Ælfwerd 30
Ælfwine 30, 929
Ælsinus (Ælfsige) 222, 591
Æþelmær 1014
Æðelric 123
Æþelric (bishop) 983
Æþelstanes (genitive) 470
Æþel 766
Æþelwerd (ealdorman) 766
Aldred 316
Aldred (bishop) 315.5
Alfuuold 379

Bald 69.6
Bealdewuine (abbot) 807
Beoffa 275
Boge (priest) 315.5
Brihtmærcild 813.8
Brihtwold 52
Byrnstan Beoffan sunu 275

Clap? 366.5
Coleman 87
Cuthsuuithae (abbess) 1044.5

Eadgar cyng 377; Æadgares cininges 771
Eadgife 367
Eadgiþ 1033
Eadryde cynigc 356.6
Eadui Basan 445
Eadwi 545
Ealdred Alfuuoldes sunu 739
Ealfric 807
Eglaf 366.5

Farmon, Færmen 812
Freoden 807

Gilebeard 839

Godmær 948.7
Godwine fax 17.5
Godwine Iustines sunu 737
Godwine mun 702

Hacun eorl 701
Hemming 172

Iustin 737

Leofred 738
Lyuinc (bishop) 1005.2

Norðman 474

Ordgiuu þeo nunne 740
Owun 813

Rodbeart 193

Sawulf 94
Siferð 156

Tate 156

Þorð Clapes sunu 366.5

Þureð 450
Þureð 472
Ðuregisel 807

Ulf 124
Ulf 366.5

Ulfcytel Osulfes sunu 474

Werburg (wife of Ealdorman Ælfred) 1021.5
Wlstan (II of Worcester) 556
Wulfgeat (not scribe of
    this manuscript) 898

Wulfgyþe 582
Wulfstan I of Worcester 537
Wulfstan of York 307
Wulfwi 530
Wulfwine 367
Wulfwine Cada 988

Index of Places

'Location' in the *Conspectus* represents a reasonable assumption of the place at which the hand was writing. It cannot take account of the mobility of scribes, nor of the fact that scribes located in one place, e.g. Cerne, may not have been trained there, as the only source of our knowledge of them (BL, Royal 7 C XII) is in a manuscript made within a few years of the foundation of the abbey (987). Reference numbers in roman are to hands placed with some degree of certainty, italic are to those less securely placed. Not all of the results of arguments which have been put forward about the location of specific scribes or groups of scribes have been included here.

Subject Index

This index is based on the listings in the Contents column of the *Conspectus*. Since that column is not intended to be comprehensive, but rather contains only an aid to the identification of the hands, it follows that the Subject Index is limited, and should be seen as a supplement to the full indexes in Ker, *Catalogue*, and Gneuss and Lapidge, *Anglo-Saxon Manuscripts*. It is included because the reader may find it useful to pursue such subjects as the number of hands glossing Aldhelm or those writing pen-trials in English.